Language Learning Online

Theory and Practice in the ESL and L2 Computer Classroom

Edited by

Janet Swaffar
Susan Romano
Phillip Markley
Katherine Arens

Labyrinth Publications
Austin, Texas

The Daedalus Group, Inc.
1106 Clayton Lane #250W
Austin, TX 78723

Language Learning Online:
Theory and Practice in the ESL and L2 Computer Classroom.
Edited by Janet Swaffar, Susan Romano, Phillip Markley, and Katherine Arens.

Library of Congress Catalog Card Number: 98-84350

ISBN 1-891430-11-4 (paperback)
ISBN 1-891430-12-2 (Electronic Format)

Senior Editor: Locke Carter
Cover design: Holli Gardner Drewry

Labyrinth Publications is dedicated to promoting high-quality scholarship at the intersection of technology and education. All printed works are also available in electronic format; visit our web site for more information:
http://labyrinth.daedalus.com/

Printed in Canada

Contents

Networking Language Learning: Introduction

Janet Swaffar

Articulate Language

Networked exchanges seem to help all individuals in language classes engage more frequently, with greater confidence, and with greater enthusiasm in the communicative process than is characteristic for similar students in oral classrooms. This volume looks at how computer networking structures language learning. As such, it presents a focus different from work on networking in English composition and literature classes. Those students who are acquiring a foreign language as an academic subject, as well as those who may be in first year English composition classes, are individuals for whom standard English or standard French, German, Spanish, or Portuguese is not the language of communication within their social environment. Social and linguistic differences result in goals and linguistic experience of minority groups and second-language learners that are unique to these groups. Despite the varied levels and instructional contexts addressed in each of the essays that follow, the thread connecting individual contributions is that computers promote articulate, extended exchanges among students who are learning to use language—their own standard language or a foreign one.

Consequently, students who are language learners focus more on structures, striving as they must to master grammatical forms with which to express rhetorical intents. Thus whereas the tendency among teachers of English composition is to reflect about theoretical goals and their discursive applications (see Slatin, this volume), language teachers focus more on linguistic structures and their sociolinguistic applications. In conjunction with this learning, teachers of language often try to recreate situations in which the cognitive and affective processes students engage in reinforce their structural learning. Here, it is presumed, computer networking may play a special, as yet unexplored, role.

Do the interactions of language learners who are networking promote particular kinds of learning? For example, is a network communication more characteristic of conversational exchanges or written ones? From a purely linguistic standpoint, do the cognitive or affective processes involved in electronic exchanges access more than previously-learned structures, or do they allow student production a new degree of freedom?

The research and examples of classroom activities presented in the chapters that follow suggest that computer "conversations" are a form of hybrid communication: while they share characteristics of spoken and written language, computer "conversations" nonetheless seem to function in a language environment very different from that of the conventional language classroom. They enable the spontaneous responses of speech and the reflective, iterative responses of writing. What effects do these differences have on language learning?

As most classroom exercises do, networking classroom exchanges commence with students' use of familiar linguistic structures. Because, however, learning curves differ, students begin to use this unique environment in personal ways. These same students' later entries in the more demanding environment of the computer InterChange (the network situation described in this volume) include experiments with unfamiliar words and usages that would hinder face-to-face conversations greatly or require much personal risk if they were attempted verbally. Classroom conversations ask students to monitor multiple communicative sign systems other than words: tone of voice, intonational patterns, phonetic variance, body language, relative position, gender and ethnicity to mention just a few. In contrast, computer exchanges ask students to monitor only words on the screen. Other factors, other distracters (voice, dress, body language), are eliminated.

Nonetheless, a different set of distracters replaces those characteristic of verbal exchanges. The high speed and multiply-threaded conversation on a network can be relatively overwhelming to the uninitiated. Language learners, however, generally do not produce the volume of prose that characterizes the average English composition class. Their more measured correspondence makes reading and writing on the network for the most part quite manageable. Reading practice reinforces fluency in very concrete ways. Command of a shared, if limited, vocabulary is reviewed and plenty of time is available for students to reflect about how to use that vocabulary to articulate their own ideas.

Too, because the computer screen offers unique visual reinforcement, as the multiple networking dialogues progress, students also begin to adopt usage and vocabulary gleaned from reading instructor and fellow classmate comments—the kind of comments that often pass one by aurally. Consequently, students who use computers tend, by the end of most sessions, to actively engage in a kind of expression not obtainable in an oral classroom.

Such findings suggest that the computer classroom is more than just a gimmick, more than an enjoyable form of language drill, but a distinctive, perhaps unique, language learning environment. The articles in this volume, whose data is drawn largely (although not exclusively) from printouts from networking classes, suggest that computers foster students' cognitive development and increasingly sophisticated expression of that development at a rate rarely attained in other learning settings.

Characteristics of Computer Classrooms

Overriding the importance of the features of individual situations, three characteristics mark the computer learning environment. As will become increasingly evident to the reader of the studies which follow, these characteristics frame each contribution's discussion. The first feature praised in every chapter is the positive student affect that seems to result from networking—the enthusiastic student response to networking activities. This enthusiasm exists even in classes where exchanges have at times been confrontational. Indeed, depending on the assignment and classroom demographics, irate or even homophobic, insensitive remarks are not uncommon in networking exchanges. Judgemental statements, however, in the experience of the authors of these essays, often prove to be the basis for committed engagement, lively discussion, and elaborated reactions that lead to more positive, less prejudicial views.

A second feature emphasized, having time to reflect about exchanges prior to participating in them, may explain why students enjoy networking more than conventional classroom conversation. Each chapter discovers independently that an oral classroom setting poses affective difficulties and frustrations for students because they find themselves unable to express their ideas as adequately in an unfamiliar idiom, register, or language as they can in their own idiolect or native language. That problem seems to be alleviated, however, in a networked classroom, through the expedient of enabling individual students to monitor before writing—to exploit a window of time and focus to gather their thoughts and linguistic abilities in order to produce successful communication. Unlike the demands for instant response inherent in verbal exchanges in oral classes, written exchanges allow time to reconsider, time to scroll down the screen and see what others have written, time to review notes or assignments brought with them to the networking class. And conversely, the computer enables immediate feedback, without the delays inherent in written feedback in the traditional classroom.

The third shared feature of computer network learning also relates to the preceding two: praise for reduced "teacher talk," resulting in greater participation among students than is characteristic in the oral classroom. Instructors no longer control 70 percent of the classroom "air time" in a networking classroom. Not only is access in terms of raw time or dominance at issue here. Often, a prime inhibitor of student engagement is a perceived ability gap between oneself and the linguistic capability of most instructors or fellow students. A particular type of spoken proficiency is a key to dominance in an oral classroom. Small wonder, then, that isolated fluent students and the teacher's instructional language skills tend to dominate oral classroom discourse. Networking classes eliminate this spoken proficiency advantage, and hence they also eliminate both the individual-student and the teacher-dominance pattern—in effect they filter out societal roles that help a forceful personality to dominate as well. On the network, because affective tricks must be encoded in writing, they are less likely to convey an emotional charge.

Thus computers minimize differences simply because a computer screen displays all entries in a single presentation format (same fonts, typescripts). Moreover, all entries appear in the order sent and are received in "natural" sequence, not stage-managed by a teacher or reconstructed from memory. Students can scroll and select entries to focus on at will. The choice is theirs.

While the instructor's linguistic command remains superior to that of the class, its affective power is reduced to being one of many, a democratizing visual perception. Without acoustic power and body language to reinforce messages, the instructor or the more fluent fellow-student becomes one among many. Such discursive equality empowers the class as a whole because the resulting atmosphere is one in which all students have an even playing field on which to express themselves—a field where sociolinguistic competence exceeds personal power.

Positive affect, reduced frustration, and sheer quantity of articulation may, nonetheless, be illusory empowerment. Unless students are learning to express themselves with increasing effectiveness (including articulateness, correctness), sheer quantity of verbiage is an insufficient measure for progress. Not only must the quantity of student production in a computer network be greater to validate it as a unique learning environment, but the quality of this production must also be. To forestall such objections, each chapter in this volume illustrates a particular aspect of the network learning environment that supports claims made here about the cognitive and linguistic benefits to be found in networking. The section that follows attempts to explain this phenomenon in overview: why students seem to be engaging in a particularly valuable learning mode when communicating in a networked classroom.

Extended Discourse in a Structured Dialogue

It would appear from the collective experience of the authors represented here that the major difference between an oral and a networking classroom is that an oral classroom is rarely able to foster extended discourse. Real-time oral work poses practical limits on conversation among participants unfamiliar with the discourse gambits that enable extended exchanges (i.e., higher-order exchanges).

Efforts to modify the more traditional classroom discussion's question / answer or move / countermove formats all suggest that classroom techniques designed to elicit varied speech acts and freer exchanges benefit students. One thinks here, for example, of research about display versus referential questions, or the impact of peer exchanges in small group work compared to commensurate teacher input. No matter the detail, networked peer exchanges do not seem to be subject to the same time (i.e., sequencing) limits of these other classroom formats

Beyond linguistic inhibitors, however, there are formidable social inhibitors of free exchanges. The language class, with one teacher and twenty to thirty students, rarely consists of students who 1) share equivalent affective responses to verbal participation, 2) have no gender or cultural prohibitions about extended verbal exchanges, 3) are visually homogenous, and 4) share equivalent verbal skills.

Without such shared social equivalencies, students in an oral classroom are generally unable to engage in extended exchanges that move smoothly from expressing viewpoints to defending and arguing them, to evaluating and synthesizing what has been discussed. Small wonder, then, that teachers rely heavily on question / answer modes and the bilateral conversations that exist are between individual students and the teacher, not among the students themselves.

Consequently, the discourse moves in oral classrooms are predominantly those of inquiry and response, no matter if they claim to be fostering "higher order discourse." Rarely is that response commented on by other students. Generally, the instructor summarizes responses and proceeds to the next point in her agenda. Thus the oral classroom discussion consists, in practice, of introductory moves (or discourse gambits) consisting of a question posed by teacher, a countering transaction on the part of one or two students who respond to the question, and a closing move on the part of the instructor who synthesizes the interaction. Such an interaction remains one-sided; the discourse gambits are set by the teacher, who thus tacitly controls the flow, no matter how liberal her intent.

Higher-Order Thinking and US Socialization

This situation, in which such a distinct hierarchy is set up in the typical US oral classroom, originates in prevailing socialization practices in this country. Socialization practices in the United States school and public environments tend to minimize exchanges in which students present and defend opinions, argue their validity, attempt to persuade others that these views need to be more broadly adopted, and synthesize stands of discussion into a coherent, rhetorically cogent evaluation. Thus the critical thinking skills we hope to encourage through classroom discussion are rarely realized practically, as options for student interaction or innovative language use in the classroom or elsewhere.

Because the US school system rarely stresses presentation of argument, counter-argument, and evaluative summaries associated with parliamentary debate orientations (more familiar in the English public school system), the affective impact of argumentation and debate on the part of American students tends to be reduced to questions of individual affect or personal impact. Such features virtually preclude that exchanges will be seen as opportunities to practice alternative verbal interactions.

It would, for example, be considered rude for John to critique Mary's assertion about a purely academic subject (e.g., an analysis of a story) or gratuitous for him to praise Mary's view, just because he felt like it. Similarly, a behavior such as questioning Mary's statement is perceived, in a North American context, as questioning that student's right to make any statement, thus as an inhibiting gesture or possibly personal attack on John's part. Thus, in an affective sense, John would be engaging in unacceptable rhetorical procedures.

Even if Mary is not to be silenced and provides a counter-argument, the resulting exchange often has a mixed classroom reception. Should such a dialogue take place in the average US classroom, it would frequently be perceived by classmates as a series of exclusionary moves, by means of which two people "take over," dominating class time and marginalizing fellow students. Because they are perceived as exclusionary, such exchanges appear to interfere with, rather than to promote, learning. And even if the "rhetorical flourishes" John is attempting are perceived, they are too readily labeled "showing off" or "going off on a tangent," not admired as models for valuable skills in discourse interaction.

From a purely practical standpoint, unless extended exchanges are structured as desirable classroom procedures, they will be viewed as asocial behaviors (as they are in, for example, presidential debates). Pragmatically speaking, it is rare that more than two or three students engage in extended exchanges. Even if, under ideal circumstances, a class of fifteen or twenty students were willing to do so, the opportunities to express themselves are limited—debaters get three to five minutes, without opportunity to structure their timing spontaneously. Similarly, consecutive natural speech allows for two or three minutes maximum for each individual, rarely sufficient time to reflect on and pursue issues in detail.

More recent pedagogical foci have suggested that small group activities can provide more time for speakers to exchange ideas and circumvent some prohibitions against perceived dominance. Unfortunately, however, while small group activities enable students to overcome their typical reluctance to speak as well as provide more real time to communicate, such exclusively oral performance often remains another kind of barrier to developing more than minimal conversational exchanges.

In small groups, questions and answers tend to predominate. Too, critical and evaluative skills are difficult to practice, particularly when, for example, foreign language students are faced with the demands inherent to spoken exchanges. On the one hand, they must engage in spontaneous response, necessitating focus on message rather than language, what is said, not how. Yet, precisely when students must use an unfamiliar language or (for them) non-standard dialect, they concentrate on monitoring linguistic features (producing rudimentary but clear sentences), or develop a group-specific physical and emotive language that patches over threadbare linguistic practices.

In effect, then, any language classroom that poses demands for spontaneous response and focus on unfamiliar usage, whether in the large-class or small-group format, will actually tend to inhibit development of critical skills in that language, especially if those skills are supposed to be linked to discourse gambits reflecting critical intent. Thoughtful commentary, like linguistic accuracy, involves the kind of reflection not possible in a real-time oral classroom—a condition emphasizing immediacy, not reflected response.

As already indicated, in order to marshal defense of opinions or persuasive reframings of arguments, students need time to think and rethink their positions and contrary positions taken. They also need to verify whether they have presented those positions clearly and strategically. That is, did speakers or writers get their messages across to others and did they do it in a way that made the impact they desired? Unless given opportunities to develop these strategies, even first language students have difficulty engaging verbally in such exchanges.

In sum, oral classrooms make unrealistic demands when they ask students to be verbally articulate in a *second* language at levels on which they rarely are asked to engage in their native dialects—a demand equally overwhelming for students switching between a native and foreign language or between a regional or local dialect variant and "standard" speech.

Correlating Critical Thinking, Speech Acts, and Semiotics

The critical skills referred to in this volume are based on the reactive processing options of the human mind: the mind's ability to understand, to reason, to imagine, and to desire (Lacan, 1977). Of these four faculties, particularly for the foreign language learner, it is the desiring faculty which teachers must first engage. Only after students want to talk, to write, to use the second language and express themselves, only then can their pursuit of language learning be taken seriously beyond the level of fulfilling minimal requirements. They must want to initiate or desire membership in a speech community.

Apparently, a networking classroom accesses student affect (or their motivational faculty) because networking facilitates a speech act many individuals find difficult in the oral classroom: inquiry (including its initiation). That inquiry is difficult in the oral classroom has to do with the affective issues addressed above. Inquiry is, however, probably also forestalled by social politeness rules that compound linguistically- and affectively-based inhibitions.

All too often, students assume others understand what they do not or that their queries concern incidentals or tangents peripheral to the thrust of classroom interaction. Also, standard culture in the United States equates interruption with bad manners (not a standard for many other cultures or many subcultures in the United States). Consequently, many questions students have are rarely posed, considered too unimportant or of only fleeting interest—students do not see that knowledge is more than "just the facts," that their need to know is an essential *part* of knowledge. In the sense that these inhibitors are reduced on the network, it encourages students to apply the desire to know to cognitive processing in an unfamiliar language.

In the networking classroom, many social constraints on affective and cognitive engagement of students disappear. A particular "speaker" is no longer demanding the floor. When the classroom participants are faced only with the computer screen full of statements from everyone in the class, focus of attention and participant response is diffused. Options for simply not paying attention are available to all participants, without the censure of a lapse in politeness. For these reasons, we conclude, computer networking is characterized by many "random" inquiries to the group as a whole, to individual classmates, or to the teacher. On a network, students are perceived as regards their linguistic demands and desires, not their affective (or intonational, physical etc.) presence.

In this light, inquiry, so often the province of the teacher in the oral classroom (and hence artificial since presumably the teacher knows the answers), is the expression of a unilateral cognitive desire to understand what someone else has expressed. Because it is unilateral, one-directional, between sender and receiver, inquiry represents a first step in cognitive processing. Particularly as revealed in the chapters by Chun and Sullivan below, inquiries play a large role in initiating exchanges. As expressions of interest in what others have to say, inquiries foster mutually-reaffirming affect (especially rhetorical affect) as well as a shared understanding, not the students' public personae.

In a classroom, opinions generally follow inquiry. This sequence seems logical from a cognitive point of view as well, because, if inquiries represent a desire to understand others, opinions express a unilateral cognitive desire to be understood by others and to project one's own understanding. The implied direction in the act of expressing an opinion is a contact from receiver to sender. Like inquiry ("What do you think?"), opinions, such as "Listen to what I think," convey a unilateral message. The direction of sender/receiver relationship and the perceived hierarchy of their abilities is reversed.

As Sullivan illustrates with her example of Marvin, the young man who initially only wanted to know what others thought, classmates' responses gave Marvin the discourse gambits he needed to express his own views (e.g., "I think that x is more important than y." or "I don't like that idea"). Ultimately, Marvin's inquiries and his tentative opinion statements encouraged verbalizations that also represented more complex cognitive processes than those involved in inquiry and opinion statements: the defense of his opinions, because the inquiries structure shared knowledge. He moved from a desire to connect, to actively understanding and defending his understanding of aspects of the selections.

Defending opinions involves juggling two perspectives: one's own and the opposition's. Hence, defense represents bilateral rather than unilateral reasoning, a still more complex cognitive activity. A student defending her opinion has to support that view in opposition to another perspective (thus tacitly balancing two points of view, logically and evaluatively). As illustrated throughout this volume, if a student engages in such cognitively more complex acts the activity almost automatically leads to increasingly sophisticated language use. Often, students move from reacting, to defending opinions with invidious comparison (i.e., to arguing overtly the superior value of those opinions). Each step requires more sophisticated discourse gambits ("Huh?" or "No," to "I like X better," to "If you'd consider X you'd see . . ." or "In that case, you would . . .")

Another example of different interactions can be illustrative of an additional difference in oral and networked classroom discourse practice. When arguing, people are no longer comparing two views, they weight their views against another person's position. Argument is more confrontational than defending an opinion.

An additional degree of cognitive sophistication is implied when students move from an explicit negative comparison (often on the level of personal opinion), to the more subtle tactics involved in persuading (and associated with rhetorical sophistication). In order to persuade, the speaker must resituate her views within the listener's frame of reference. To continue with the earlier example, John might have presented his counter-argument to Mary's belief that American's are seen as a peace-loving nation with a persuasively-constructed hypothetical statement such as "If you think about the amount of violence shown in American movies distributed overseas, then you'll see why people all over the world think Americans are violent." The invitation to consider an alternative point of view (negative attitudes towards Americans) is aligned with a rational basis for considering that point of view (the reactions of people in other countries to violence in the American films they view).

Ultimately, as a complex cognitive act, the discursive ability to align two perspectives (those of other countries, those of American-made movies shown in those countries) recasts the unidentified views of others in the speaker's frame of reference or imagined alternatives. Such a task involves more than wanting to be understood. Understanding (the speaker's position on an issue) must be linked to subject matter (the external evidence drawn into the speaker's discourse), since the speaker is renegotiating a situation or state of affairs (challenging the idea that others are misguided or ignorant to view Americans as violent), not only pointing towards a new positive or negative evaluation of known combinations of facts (violence in American movies does/does not represent a linked chain of reasoning that explains international perceptions of Americans as real people).

No claim can be made at this juncture that networking leads to incrementally more sophisticated discourse management. What the contributions in this volume do suggest, however, is that the linguistic and affective gains cited seem to be anchored in a discursive modality that encourages greater freedom of expression, increased tendencies to substantiate claims, and enhanced curiosity about why fellow students express themselves the way they do.

At very least, such intellectual curiosity predisposes students toward becoming more articulate. Ultimately, however, we want more than increasingly articulate students. We want students who are learning how to express themselves about significant issues. To do that, a sound analysis must be rooted in substantive information. In order to do things with words, students have to have something to say.

Higher-Order Thinking and Subject Matter

The structure of this volume assumes a linkage between rhetorical and cognitive development, and demonstrates how that development is enabled by the extended discourse options in a networking environment. All example exchanges discussed in this volume encourage students to express their ideas—ostensibly a free-writing task. But that task is by no means subjectively free, because students share a concept of the network environment—as a place to think in unfamiliar language about relatively unfamiliar ideas, information, and message systems in assigned texts.

In these chapters, students express views about material read in preparation for the networked class. That referentiality is an important limit on "free" writing (in the sense of completely subjective and hence self-perpetuating language use). Because it is the classroom referent, the text models vocabulary, grammar, discourse gambits, and ideas accessible to the networked student in two dimensions: as individual readers and the text, and as individual readers' understanding of the text vis-à-vis one another.

With its heightened reflective potential and affectively-neutralized communicative structure, the networked class can address text dimensions that promote cognitive and linguistic development. Consequently, resulting speech acts (the discourses students were encouraged to produce) are informed by a database, the language and views expressed in a text. Thus, although students are freely and spontaneously exchanging ideas, the source and fulcrum for those ideas remains objectively verifiable. In this sense, the networking exchanges are, from the standpoint of subject matter, *not* free writing tasks.

In virtually all of the documented discussions, inquiry and expression of opinion are viewed as important entry-level stages in understanding text meaning, because asking for information and assuming positions vis-à-vis classroom information indicates that students attend to textual subject matter, thus giving the designated linguistic data-base preeminence over their own linguistic ability or personal-affective concerns. This focus aids them in crossing that combination of affective and cognitive thresholds which must be surmounted before their reasoning processes can be engaged on more sophisticated discourse gambits (defending opinions, projecting). Students must explore what they think the text says before they analyze why they hold these views.

Inquiry and opinion statements form the foundation for crossing what may be considered a semantic as well as a cognitive and linguistic threshold: focusing on the semantics of classroom content, before engaging in reasoning (a syntactically-driven process) about those semantics. Initially, semantics inform students' cognitive processes and their verbalized inquiry and opinion about texts: the who, what, where, and when of subject matter discussed by the class.

In the case of a regional or social usage variant, for example, two facts of contemporary language use often run afoul of each other in the language classroom. For example, standard grammar upheld within the social concept offered by the non-standard usage ("I don't think Black English is a language" or "African-Americans who use that language are uneducated") can be an effective rhetorical gambit that intimidates or angers those arguing for the validity of an alternative. That gambit creates barriers to communication by invalidating a discourse about language. Here, again, the computer can aid in distinguishing semantics (the computer has no color, hairstyle, or accent) of social power from linguistic ability.

As already indicated, the links between the unilateral affective and the cognitive levels of understanding through inquiry and opinion assertion, once established, seem to lay the foundation for increasingly complex speech acts that juxtapose sender / receiver systems (i.e., bilateral cognitive moves). The importance of soccer in South America can remain the semantic focus whether inquiries address the receiver ("what was the last time Argentina won the World Cup?") or opinions represent the sender ("I think soccer is important because it gives Third World countries a change to be winners"). Regardless of the sender / receiver relationship, soccer has remained the pivotal semantic sign system in these two exchanges. Only the direction of the call for understanding has shifted.

Bilateral exchanges, as described, add cognitive complexity to the communication because the linguistic demands are higher when one is not just expressing opinions, but defending a opinion (comparing two perspectives about the game of soccer), arguing a position (ways to reduce the violence often associated with the game), or persuading (reframing another's argument about the reasons soccer fans get carried away).

In order to pursue new avenues of thought or investigate their capacity to express original insights, students need to synthesize information from multiple sources. Discussions about current events, for example, must be raised from the level of opposing opinions held by particular individuals to the status of an issue containing information which may be reassembled by all participants, albeit framed from different individuals' perspectives. When students are asked to discuss a question relating to an essay or a story, their variously-formulated answers can even be used in subsequent class sessions to point out different framings (e.g., a feminist, economic, political, or social perspective).

Computer exchanges thus facilitate such transformations of opinions to issues, because they ease stages in development toward higher-order thinking and the more sophisticated rhetoric such discourse situations require (specific logical speech acts). They document extended discourse about a shared system of signs, the language of subject matter presented in the instructional syllabus. Many students have arguments to substantiate their claims, but have not learned to articulate those arguments (or not in standard language).

One important use for networking transcripts is to extrapolate those statements that make arguments explicit and have students see the difference between an implied (covert) argument and a stated one. In the example above, the difference would be illustrated in those student statements that simply describe the behavior of a figure in a story, thereby only implying an argument ("He would only dance with pretty girls" or "He thought small town girls were beneath him") and those that render explicit the connection between social, gender-based, or economic factors and the origins of the protagonist's bias.

Such explicit statements might, for instance, analyze the basis for the hero's prejudices in the following terms: "In rejecting the girls at the party as insufficiently attractive, the protagonist reveals he sees only their value as objects: pretty or not pretty." Reading excerpts from their exchanges, students are given the chance to identify and discuss the substantiated (overtly argued) and the purely descriptive (covertly argued) answers in order to reflect about this distinction.

Higher-Order Strategies and Linguistic Structures

In effect, then, this volume documents that computer exchanges promote formal linguistic accuracy precisely because they allow students to engage in more varying speech acts, representing their affective commitment, yet driven by different levels of sophisticated cognition in a range from less to more sophisticated linguistic or rhetorical structures. Styles of inquiring, arguing, persuading, and evaluating presented here as part of student output in networked classrooms demonstrate that networking seems to foster extended discourse scenarios. These scenarios come about because, in networking, four faculties of mind—desire, understanding, reasoning, and imagining—can develop through reflection in an affectively neutral linguistic environment (Lacan). Said another way, given a networking format, students develop linguistic skills because they can recycle language in cognitively (and, hence, syntactically) more complex ways, without socially-based inhibitions.

Participants use the same semantics when they move from one speech act to the next, but the relationships between those semantics change as they progress from initiating unilateral conversational moves to bilateral exchanges. Moreover, students need not move in those stages precipitously or under duress. They can reflect about what they are going to say, read it and revise it before sending their communication. They can monitor through reading and rereading the statements of others. If still hesitant, participants can elect not to play, to disengage from exchanges that appear cognitively, affectively, or linguistically unproductive for them.

The Sense of the Network

The purpose of this volume is to substantiate the claims made above by presenting representative work on networking classes—to demonstrate how the network creates a distinctive learning environment, to describe the advantages of that environment for teaching, and, finally, to suggest areas of research appropriate for the future and ways to implement networking into any language curriculum.

The contributions have been grouped in sections that address the pieces of this agenda:

Section I offers a single contribution by John Slatin, who describes how the Daedalus InterChange classroom is set up and details the complex and shifting institutional circumstances, coupled with faculty and graduate student initiative, that facilitated the teaching and research described in the following essays.

Section II presents three studies that examine characteristics of linguistic output attributable to networking. Sullivan looks at how exchanges frequently address the affectively-based communicative problems often found in a multi-ethnic English language classroom. She shows how networking discussions of reading assignments develop increasingly sophisticated expression among all participants. Chun demonstrates that students beginning foreign language study develop discourse skills in their weekly networking sessions that, while closely paralleling those learned in the oral classroom, reveal features unique to networking. Markley's chapter compares the behaviors of student groups in English composition classes for non-native speakers, in order to assess how a networking environment can influence students' engagement and outcomes when behavior is predicated on the gender and ethnic background.

Section III presents two studies that document student reactions to the network. Beauvois assesses her opinion survey, consisting of pre- and post-semester interviews and student questionnaires, to establish how students' attitudes toward themselves as learners change significantly as a result of a weekly networking session, and to show that students perceive many of the same advantages of networking that research has identified. Also addressing attitudes, Jaeglin's study elaborates results like Beauvois' by comparing student and instructor attitudes and their preferences for computer use, and by expanding the student sample to include both lower-division (first- and second-year) language students and upper-division ones.

Section IV explores alternative ways to use networking. Kelm describes how to set up, monitor, and structure an international and / or local e-mail system for intermediate students of Portuguese. Kelm shows how to implement assignments on the Internet to enrich student's exposure to foreign culture and language by engaging in regular correspondence. Swaffar considers how the nature of L2 research will probably change as a result of the options available through networking, offering a case study in evaluating discourse. Her proposal that essays be assessed as regards four levels of discourse complexity can be used in feedback to students, as a template for course design, or as one standard to evaluate student progress.

Finally, a brief set of concluding remarks suggests what the results collected here imply for the future of research and teaching in the networked classroom—not as the latest technological gimmick, but as a valid part of carefully structured teaching and learning environments.

References

Lacan, J. (1977). The subversion of the subject and the dialectic of desire in the Freudian unconscious. In *Écrits. A Selection.* (pp. 292-325). New York: W. W. Norton.

Section 1

Marrying Technology to the Liberal Arts

Section I is a single contribution by John Slatin describing how the Daedalus InterChange classroom, material foundation of the teaching and research represented in this volume, evolved from a condition of marginalized eccentricity and tenuous attachment to the English Department, to become the centerpiece of the University of Texas at Austin's Division of Rhetoric and Composition. Slatin presents a narrative of software development and institutional politics cross-referenced with dedication to the teaching of writing on the one hand and entrepreneurial enterprise on the other. He offers a template for those interested in software development and pedagogical applications, demonstrating how state-of-the-art technical expertise was used to achieve a product and a practice that came to function quite differently from what was originally envisioned, and came finally to serve publics in ways not entirely foreseen by its progenitors. This story suggests that deans, funding agencies, and department chairs can become strong allies in the search for applied technologies.

Yet the very successes imply caution. Slatin leaves to the academic reader's schemata details of time commitment and frustration. Funded by the campus entity called Project QUEST, his personal path from literary critic to software producer to laboratory administer of a major composition studies program at the University of Texas was a quest indeed. His initial project, developing a computer program for the visually impaired, undergoes a series of seemingly unrelated transformations: from working with tutorial software designed to train military personnel in equipment use, to learning about programs serving the needs of the deaf community at Gallaudet, to applying rhetorical and linguistic theory to a software program intended initially for remedial courses in English composition, and culminating (for the time being) in leading the development of computer applications for teaching writing at the University of Texas. He witnesses and underwrites, thus, a metamorphosis of teaching writing at Texas.

Throughout this narrative of converging impulses, a shift occurs in the type of minority audiences served. Deaf and blind students are, at this writing, no longer the focus of attention, quite simply because, in the main, those are not the primary audiences served by the University. Other more traditional "minority" groups on campus have, however, been quick to see the advantages for their programs, in particular ESL students and students in foreign languages. While initial indicators suggest that on-line communication offers significant benefits to classrooms of all kinds, the bulk of published research to date has been drawn from data on composition in English. This volume, although it focuses primarily on the responses of second and foreign language learners to on-line communication in the classroom, locates that enterprise in the larger picture of changes taking place across North American universities and colleges at this time. Faculty confronted with the task of implementing computer tools literally cannot do it alone. Outside expertise, teamwork, and flexibility are inherent to success. Further, as stressed in this piece, that teamwork will tend to be interdisciplinary. Faculties will be working across fields to avoid reinventing the wheel, on the one hand, and to synthesize ideas from various sources on the other.

Thus, while this volume foregrounds what second-language teachers, their students, and their pedagogies have to offer, it does so in terms of the broad academic community working towards good pedagogical use of computer software in the liberal arts. Consequently, this collection begins with a chapter in Section I reviewing how technologies can enable faculty, administrators, and instructors to envision the location and relocation of computers in an academic, institutional setting.

The Computer Writing and Research Lab: A Brief Institutional History

John Slatin

Introduction

The essays in this volume describe efforts by faculty at the University of Texas at Austin to develop a network-based pedagogy which re-orients computer-assisted language learning (CALL) away from drill-and-practice applications modeled on print-based workbooks and toward a social-interactive model of second-language acquisition. This pedagogical transformation is closely related to a movement taking place in writing instruction across the United States, a movement in which the Computer Writing and Research Lab (CWRL) at the University of Texas at Austin has played a leading role. Increasingly, college and university writing programs are setting up networked computer classrooms, in which student writers and instructors develop both increasing fluency and increasing rhetorical skill in addressing real audience by writing to and for one another over the network.

Daedalus InterChange®

The software that enables this dynamic new practice is the InterChange module of the Daedalus Integrated Writing Environment (DIWE). InterChange, which runs on Macintoshes or PC-compatibles connected to a local area network (LAN), is a very simple program which belongs to the genre of "real-time" conferencing software, meaning that, unlike e-mail, where communication is asynchronous, all InterChange participants are logged in to the network at the same time.

The InterChange screen is divided into two parts. The bottom portion is a private composing "window" where participants write what they wish to say, usually starting with replies to a prompt posted by the instructor at or just before the beginning of class and then, later, in response to their classmates' remarks as well as other comments by the instructor. When they are finished writing, they press the "Send" button and their messages are "published" to the transcript window in the upper portion of the screen; this is a scrolling list which displays all the messages in chronological order. The design of the software eliminates the usual conversational turn-taking and allows all participants to write simultaneously, while each one works at his or her own pace.

While it might sound as though classes would inevitably degenerate into collections of individuals working without reference to the larger context of the class, in fact the opposite tends to be true. This seemingly paradoxical situation, in which everyone "speaks" at once while "speaking" privately, encourages much higher levels of participation than is generally possible in traditional classroom environment. Furthermore, these InterChange sessions may have a more lasting effect than is possible for the typical oral session in class. When the discussion is over, instructors may print out and distribute complete or partial transcripts, using them as the basis of further written work or oral exercises that take their point of departure from the students' own utterances.

Institutional Structures

I will leave it to my colleagues to explain how they and their students have used InterChange and other software to enhance second-language learning. The point I wish to make and amplify here is that the pedagogical developments described in this volume are not and cannot be isolated phenomena. They require institutional structures different from those sustaining and sustained by traditional pedagogies. Since those structures are often lacking, at least in part, at many institutions, including this one, they have to be created. This is not a simple process, and it may be a painful one as well; major cultural transformations can't help but be wrenching. So what I want to do here is to tell at least part of the story of the environment that gave rise to what is now the Daedalus Integrated Writing Environment—and the way in which our deepening exploration of the pedagogical possibilities offered by this and other software has transformed the institution.

The University of Texas at Austin

The Division of Rhetoric and Composition, a new institutional structure established in June 1993, will pursue an aggressive plan of computerizing writing instruction at the University of Texas at Austin. By 1999, we will be teaching approximately 85 per cent of our undergraduate writing courses on-line. Second-language instruction seems likely to follow a similar course. As the essays in this collection report, the results obtained by second-language learners in computer-assisted classes are comparable to those we have seen with computer-based writing instruction for native speakers, and the College of Liberal Arts is now actively developing plans for more extensive integration of computer technology into second-language instruction. Thus the experience of the CWRL may offer useful models or guides for colleagues in other fields. The story of how the CWRL came to occupy its current place is a somewhat tangled one, however, in which personal initiative, institutional and disciplinary structures, and practices converge, and the details may play out differently in other fields and on other campuses. I will do my best to highlight what seem to me the more generalizable aspects of the case, but readers will have to judge for themselves how or whether the narrative presented here applies to the situations in which they find themselves.

Computers in English Departments

I have suggested elsewhere (Slatin, 1992) that the emergence of contemporary critical theory as the dominant discourse within English Studies is to some extent an effect indirectly produced by the introduction of the computer as a new "defining technology" (Bolter, 1984) in the industrialized economies. The visible presence of computers in departments of English is something else again, however, and results from a combination of factors: individual decisions, administrative pressure for efficiency, and corporate and university imperatives to develop and develop markets for new technologies. There is also a broader cultural imperative to develop structures that will assist in the transition from print to an information-based economy.

Project QUEST

An on-going initiative called Project QUEST has been one of the principal means by which computers entered the University of Texas English Department. The IBM Corporation, seeking to expand the potential uses and market for its new and wildly successful personal computers (first released in 1981, they quickly established a *de facto* industry standard), and extrapolating from the model of the successful Athena project at the Massachusetts Institute of Technology (Turkle, 1992), donated millions of dollars worth of microcomputers to the University of Texas at Austin and other US universities.[1] These were distributed to faculty who submitted proposals outlining innovative uses of microcomputers in instruction and research.

I had written a successful proposal (1985) to develop expertise in using word processing software together with synthetic speech to help visually impaired writers, including myself, work more independently. I taught my first computer-assisted writing class for visually impaired students in the summer of 1986, using software I had written myself, with mixed but generally positive results. As I was trying to improve the clumsy software I had written, I ran into a programming problem I was unable to resolve. I sought help from my colleague Jerome Bump, a specialist in Victorian literature who had written another successful QUEST proposal dealing with possible uses of computers to enhance creativity. Bump in turn asked one of his graduate students, Fred Kemp—now Director of Composition at Texas Tech University in Lubbock, Texas—to come over and help me out.

Visiting the Computer Research Lab

My conversation with Kemp led to my first visit to the basement of the Undergraduate Library, where he and several other graduate students were creating what they grandly called a "computational classroom," arranging 24 networked IBM PCs neatly in rows in the manner of a traditional theater-style classroom. They had designated another room across the hall as the Computer Research Lab. Thus what is now the CWRL was established almost casually as a by-product of Bump's successful proposal to Project QUEST.[2]

The Bump-Burns Seminar

This small group of students had originally been brought together by a seminar on rhetoric and computers which Bump co-taught in the Fall 1986 with Lt. Col. Hugh Burns of the Intelligent Systems Division at Brooks Air Force Base in San Antonio.[3] Burns had received his Ph.D. from the University of Texas at Austin in 1979, having written the first doctoral dissertation in what is now the field of Computers and Writing (Burns, 1979). His dissertation project centered on a program called TOPOI, written in BASIC for the DEC-10 mainframe computer. TOPOI was an ambitious effort to go beyond the notion of the computer as a kind of infinitely patient workbook that dominated early conceptions of the computer as "teaching machine." The program would engage the student in "dialogue" about a proposed writing project, presenting a prompt based on the work of classical and twentieth-century rhetoricians (Aristotle, Kenneth Burke, and Becker, Young, and Pike); it would then "evaluate" the student's response and "decide" which prompt to offer next on the basis of the student's response. The natural language processing required for such a project to succeed is far beyond the capacities of the BASIC programming language and remains an elusive goal of artificial intelligence research. But as an invention heuristic—that is, a program designed to assist students in developing and exploring a possible essay topic—TOPOI accorded well with a new model of writing instruction that was then achieving prominence (see below), and it provided the "seed" for what became the Computer Research Lab. By the time of the seminar in 1986, Burns had become an expert on the design of artificially intelligent tutoring systems used by the Air Force to train aircraft mechanics, but he had continued to play an important role in the emerging field of Computers and Writing.

The Process Model of Writing

The graduate students from the Bump/Burns seminar had continued working together after the seminar was over, developing software to address specific issues in the teaching of writing. At first, they designed programs in accordance with the "process approach" to writing instruction. This is a cognitively-oriented model that focuses primarily on the processes of individual student writers as they plan, compose, and revise, moving back and forth recursively among the different activities. Evolving from the work of Janet Emig (1971) and Linda Flower and John Hayes (1980, 1981), the process approach had become a dominant model for writing instruction across the United States by the early 1980s. The process model replaced the current-traditional model (Berlin, 1987) whose focus on grammatical and mechanical "correctness" had dominated writing instruction in the United States since the late nineteenth century. This paradigm shift (Hairston, 1982), with its dramatic emphasis on revision as a crucial component of successful writing, coincided with the development of word processing software, especially for micro (that is, personal) computers, which provided a practical means for accomplishing the revision activities called for by the instructional model. More subtly but no less importantly, the cognitivist orientation of the process model had roots in computational models of mind developed during the 1970s.[4]

The first programs developed in the Computer Research Lab supported specific aspects of the writing process: Fred Kemp's *Idealog* adapted Burns's TOPOI to the IBM PC and focused on invention or pre-writing, while Paul Taylor's *Descant* assisted revision by automating a response worksheet developed by Maxine Hairston. But the process model itself was already being challenged. Other programs developed in the Computer Research Lab—Locke Carter's *In-Class Mail* and Paul Taylor's *Forum*[5]—sought to implement an alternative approach advocated by Kenneth Bruffee (1984) and others, a social-epistemic (Berlin, 1987) rhetorical approach rooted in the Vygotskian conception that knowledge of reality, and indeed to some extent reality itself, emerges through and is dependent upon social interaction.[6] What was remarkable was not only that both types of software worked and worked well; it was even more remarkable that these programs, used together, reconciled with seeming effortlessness two orientations to writing and to knowledge that many researchers have regarded as seriously at odds.

The Daedalus Integrated Writing Environment

What is now called the Daedalus Integrated Writing Environment, or DIWE, is a suite of applications designed to integrate different aspects of the writing process, allowing a dynamic interplay of individual and collaborative work. Besides a simple word processor and a small bibliographic database, DIWE consists of four core modules, two of them closely allied with the process model and two oriented toward collaborative learning. *Invent* guides students through systematic exploration of possible essay topics, while *Respond* takes them through the process of responding constructively to classmates' draft essays. From my perspective, however, DIWE's great power derives from the two social-constructionist/ collaborative modules. *Mail* is an "asynchronous" messaging system akin to computer bulletin board systems, and *InterChange* is a "real-time conferencing system" that permits students and instructors to engage in "live" discussion by sending written messages over the computer network so that they appear in a "transcript window" on each participant's screen; class members respond to messages that interest them or propose new topics.

InterChange, in particular, radically transforms classroom dynamics (Butler, 1992; Taylor, 1993; Slatin, 1992). Because the software eliminates traditional conversational turn-taking and permits everyone to write simultaneously, it enables a significantly greater rate of participation, resulting in a richer, more complex discussion than is usually possible in traditional classroom environments; it is not uncommon for participation to approach 100 per cent (Slatin, 1992). The program also produces printed transcripts, which may be sorted either chronologically or alphabetically by participant.

Impact of the Daedalus Integrated Writing Environment

This software is exerting a revolutionary impact on writing instruction: DIWE is now in use at more than 500 two- and four-year colleges and universities, and a number of high schools, in the United States and more than 16 countries around the world. The software has achieved this impact as a commercial product,[7] and it is at least arguable that it could not have achieved such widespread dissemination otherwise. The Daedalus Integrated Writing Environment and other computer-based instructional software are also proving valuable in second-language instruction, whether the target language be English (as in France, for example) or Spanish, French, or German. The remaining essays in this volume describe a variety of pedagogical experiments involving computer-assisted language learning, concentrating particularly on DIWE's role. But none of these important pedagogical innovations will realize their full potential without corresponding changes in the institutional infrastructure, for teaching in the computer-based classroom is profoundly different from teaching in more traditional environments.

The Computer Research Lab

I became director of the Computer Research Lab (CRL) in January, 1989, a year and a half after I started teaching in the graduate students' computational classroom. My goal as director was a limited one: I wanted to create an environment that would permit and indeed nurture a recurrence of the creative explosion that had happened serendipitously with the original group of graduate students. For I believed that the phenomenon could be replicated if the conditions were right. But creating the right conditions was, and is, a more difficult proposition than I realized at first.

I had expected to work within the existing cultural and institutional framework—that is, I saw the Lab as a small but important part of the English Department, a place for innovative, slightly off-beat work that would nevertheless contribute to the preservation of mainstream cultural institutions like poetry, the field where my own early research had concentrated. Like most people in comparable situations, that is, I understood myself as promoting a change of method in the interest of accomplishing more effectively the goals my colleagues and I had been pursuing previously. I was wrong, however, in some very fundamental respects. Indeed, it is at least arguable that the creation of the Division of Rhetoric and Composition in 1993 was in part a by-product of the presence of the Computer Research Lab. As Sproull and Kiesler (1991) and others have pointed out, introducing new communication technologies into existing organizations for purposes of increased efficiency often leads to unanticipated systemic effects, such as changes in the way the organization defines itself and its objectives (see also Zuboff, 1988).

As I mentioned earlier, Project QUEST awarded computers to faculty on the strength of competitive proposals. But Project QUEST also awarded computers on condition that faculty members' departments make commitments to provide necessary support for their projects. Such support might involve maintenance, personnel for programming work that faculty members couldn't do themselves, or—crucially—space, as in the original *Star Trek* (space is the final frontier on many campuses). Once the project was judged successful (or at least on the road to success), the equipment would be transferred from Project QUEST's inventory to the inventory of the faculty member's home department. It thus became necessary for the local institution to evolve structures, if it didn't already have them, to accommodate these projects—and to accommodate the presence of computers.

All this is retrospective, of course: I didn't see it at the time, but it occurs to me now that the CRL *was* just such a structure, at least where my own department was concerned; indeed, I would like to think that it has served a broader purpose as one of the structures evolved by the field of

English Studies as a whole to handle the movement of computers, not just into a single department but into the discipline as well. This is a complex issue, however: despite the presence of a substantial number of computers on faculty desks in the English Department, most members of the department remain indifferent to instructional uses of the technology, and the departmental computer committee voted against building a computer classroom for literature classes as recently as last Spring. But I am getting ahead of myself again. My concerns in the Spring of 1989 were far more localized.

When I took over direction of the CRL, there were just four lower-division writing courses meeting in the computational classroom, all of them on an *ad hoc* basis because there was no way either to schedule classes for the computer classroom or to designate particular sections as computer-assisted: the Department didn't really have any official awareness of the Lab. By another *ad hoc* arrangement, the people teaching those classes were in effect serving as Teaching Assistants for one another, providing what support they could in keeping equipment going and helping students and instructors figure out what to do and how to solve day-to-day or even moment to moment problems in the classroom.

The first problem I tackled, therefore, was to get the CRL and the computer classroom into the regular departmental scheduling process. This would make it possible to regularize appointments to the CRL so that graduate students could be assigned to teach there and so that there would be enough of them to staff the facility while classes were in session; it would also make it possible to collect fees from students taking computer-assisted courses through the CRL, just as other departments on campus did.

The Staffing Model

The Lab has been administered by the Division of Rhetoric and Composition since June 1993, and we have formalized the *ad hoc* arrangement whereby instructors provide practical support for one another. I believe it has been crucial to the success of what is now the Computer Writing and Research Lab (CWRL). As of this writing (February 1995), we offer more than 30 computer-assisted classes a semester, most of them taught by graduate student Assistant Instructors (AI's). These AI's are assigned to the CWRL for a full year; their appointments require that they teach one course per semester and work an additional seven hours per week as members of the Lab staff. Staff work involves both routine classroom support and participation in on-going Lab projects such as the development of computer-based instructional materials (courseware) and documentation, as well as identification and documentation of successful pedagogical practices and research into other pedagogical applications of computer technology.

Rationale for the Staffing Model

There are several reasons for doing it this way. First, pedagogically informed technical support is an essential component of successful computer-assisted teaching and learning, especially in environments like the Daedalus classroom, where intensive and fast-paced personal interaction is mediated by and dependent upon computer use. That is, support staff should understand and share the instructors' pedagogical goals, recognizing the impact of technical arrangements on learning and instruction (by contrast, computer services staff are often focused primarily upon the technology). Many students—and instructors—lack the technical skills necessary to solve technical problem as they arise, especially at the beginning of the semester, when technical failures can exacerbate intellectual doubts; but even technologically knowledgeable students and instructors should be free to concentrate on subject matter and course work.

This staffing arrangement has other important advantages also, making the Lab a learning environment for the graduate students as well as the undergraduates whom they are directly responsible for teaching. The graduate students "learn the classroom" from two perspectives at once—that of the teacher and that of the support staff—and see firsthand what it takes to maintain an effective instructional environment. They also become members of a small but growing community within the department, entering an ongoing conversation about computer-based teaching in particular and about teaching in general that extends beyond the Lab to include others in the department.[8]

Expansion and Development

The second problem I wanted to address when I became director of the CRL was to replace our aging equipment[9] and to expand our facilities to meet the rising demand I anticipated. This too was a drawn-out process, and remains a continuing concern. Late in the Fall of 1987, Bump and I were invited to make a presentation to the Liberal Arts Faculty Computer Committee about the work we had been doing in the CRL under the Project QUEST grant. The Liberal Arts Faculty Computer Committee was dominated by people doing quantitative research in the social sciences, who had little familiarity either with writing instruction or with computer applications outside their own areas of expertise—except, of course, for basic word processing. Our emphasis on pedagogical innovation and development of cutting-edge software elicited considerable surprise, therefore, and then-Associate Dean Joseph Horn, a psychologist, suggested that I prepare a five-year plan for departmental computing in English. W.O.S. Sutherland, who was chair of the English Department at the time, authorized me to go forward.

National Survey

The previous summer (1987), on my own initiative but with departmental support in the form of postage, I had conducted an unscientific national survey of computer usage in departments of English.[10] On the strength of that survey, I was convinced that our department was in many respects more heavily computerized than most, with the possible exception of Carnegie-Mellon. The average English department in my 1987 survey had 23 personal computers or terminals on its inventory; we had 37 at that time, plus another 38 located in the CRL itself. Even without the CRL computers, we were "ahead" of the mainstream.

I shared my survey data with a small group of colleagues on a newly appointed departmental committee. They agreed with me that the department should attempt to maintain and enhance its leadership in this area, and with their approval I wrote a report that recommended the following: (1) installing network connections for all faculty members; (2) hosting a national or international conference on computers and the humanities; (3) building a second computer classroom for the department, this one to be Macintosh-based; and (4) creating a large text database of materials that could be used in computer-assisted literary analysis.

The Pedagogical Text Archive

We are just now, as I write, completing the first objective, installing network connections in faculty offices in the Department of English and the Division of Rhetoric and Composition (founded in 1993 to assume responsibility for undergraduate writing instruction at the University of Texas at Austin). Other objectives were met more quickly, however. In February of 1989, for example, I was able with the help of Larry Carver, a colleague who was then working as an assistant to UT System Chancellor Hans Mark, to secure a small grant to buy another computer with a large hard drive to support the large text database project;[11] I had also been able to get funds from the College of Liberal Arts to buy a Kurzweil scanner.[12] As it happens, however, the database we have created is not a database of literary texts, as I had anticipated it would be: that work is going on at other institutions (University of Virginia, Oxford, Toronto, Georgetown, and Rutgers, for example). Instead, we have assembled a unique collection of computer-based, pedagogically-related materials composed by students and instructors. This archive consists of InterChange transcripts, draft essays, completed essays, assignment files, messages posted to the classrooms' electronic bulletin boards, and other materials created over the years in conjunction with teaching in the computer classroom; this enormously valuable record of changing pedagogical practices and linguistic habits now runs to well over a gigabyte, over 100,000 pages and millions of words. A comparable archive of materials related to and generated in the process of second-language instruction might be of considerable value.

The Sixth Conference on Computers and Writing

We met our second goal in the Spring of 1990 by co-hosting, with Texas Tech University where Fred Kemp was by then teaching, the Sixth Conference on Computers and Writing. It was at that conference, in May 1990, that many in the Computers and Writing community first clearly saw the connections between network-based writing instruction on the Daedalus or ENFI model (Batson, 1988, 1993), and other research in hypertext, which is, if you like, a kind of networked writing. As Gail Hawisher, co-editor of the journal *Computers and Composition*, exclaimed following a brilliant panel by Stuart Moulthrop, John McDaid, and Terry Harpold, "It's all one!"

The Search for Funding

Meanwhile, I continued looking for money to establish a second computer classroom. The opportunity came in the Fall of 1989, when the Liberal Arts Faculty Computer Committee solicited departmental proposals. It was at this point that computer-assisted second-language instruction at the University of Texas got a major boost. I initially went in with a proposal to enhance and expand the CRL by replacing existing equipment and setting up a second classroom. Dean Standish Meacham asked me, however, to re-think my proposal on broader scale: he and the Provost were particularly interested in creating interdepartmental computing facilities that could take maximum advantage of the capital investment in computers. I was asked in particular to incorporate the languages into my proposal. This was something of a shock: like most English professors in the United States, I thought of English as a *literary* discipline whose intellectual affinities lay to a considerable extent with the social sciences. From the College perspective, however, English evidently appeared as a language department, like French/Italian, Spanish/Portuguese, or Germanic Languages, and the Dean wanted a proposal that would give body, computationally speaking, to that conception.

Humanities and Language Computing Proposal

I then wrote a proposal to establish a Center for Humanities and Language Computing, or CHALC, which I envisioned as a set of computer classrooms and labs[13] in a wheel-like arrangement with the Computer Research Lab at the hub of the wheel and facilities in Classics, the Language Labs, and English connected to the hub by the campus ethernet. The Center would be run by a faculty Director supported by an interdepartmental faculty committee, and the CRL itself would be staffed by graduate students from participating departments. The budget for that proposal was $650,000. The proposal was approved. I was not allowed to use the word "Center," however—the Provost did not favor creating new Centers at that time—and the administrative and staffing arrangements I had envisioned were never implemented, so that individual departments proceeded on their own once equipment had been purchased and installed.

Funding came in two installments, a year apart. In the spring of 1991, we received $300,000 for the initial phase. (At the time I thought that would be the entire allocation.) Fortunately, prices had come down so much since I drafted the original proposal that I was able to do much (though not all) of what I had originally planned to do. With that money (and after several months of negotiating with representatives from IBM), I was able to replace the original IBM PCs, by then ancient and failing, with new IBM PS/2 model 70's, at the same time setting up the second, Macintosh-based computer classroom that I had proposed to my colleagues in English in 1988; I was also able to furnish the Computer Research Lab itself with a mixture of more powerful PS/2's and Macintoshes and with a NeXT workstation, a UNIX-based machine which has since become a very important part of our operation.[14] At the same time, I purchased a number of Macintoshes for the Classics Department, whose faculty were then beginning to experiment with the Perseus Project's hypermedia materials on ancient Greek civilization and language. In addition, I was able to set up a small network in the language labs—fifteen workstations for use by the language departments. I also arranged for the Language Lab to get a copy of the then brand-new Macintosh version of the Daedalus software, then called *DIScourse*, which we were also testing in the CRL's new Macintosh classroom. These facilities came on-line in time (just) for the beginning of the Fall 1991 semester.

Establishing the CRL as a Departmental Presence

Much to my surprise, I received an additional $250,000 the following year, bringing the total allocation for 1991-92 and 1992-93 to $550,000. Prices had continued to fall, of course,[15] so again the money went farther than I had anticipated two years earlier. I began by planning a multimedia lab in Parlin Hall, the building where most English faculty offices are located and where most English classes are taught. I had two goals in doing this. First, I wanted to establish the CRL as a physical presence in department, to make faculty and graduate students more aware of the work we were doing and encourage them to join in the effort. Second, I wanted a way to connect the building to the campus-wide network backbone, which would otherwise have been impossible. At UT Austin, the Computation Center pays for bringing the network cable within reach of each building, but individual departments are responsible for funding their actual network connections; this $13,000 cost was well beyond the capacities of the English Department's operating budget.

Multimedia was the major theme of the remaining purchases that year. Besides the CRL's new multimedia lab, we were also able to buy additional equipment to support the Classics Department's continuing efforts to integrate the Perseus Project and other software into the curriculum, and, at the Dean's request, to bring the American Studies new multimedia efforts into the project. We provided additional support for computer-assisted language learning as well, supplying multimedia equipment requested by the Language Labs and several additional workstations to bring their complement up to 20, enough for a class of respectable size.

The Division of Rhetoric and Composition

Perhaps inevitably, there were delays in installing network ports and new electrical wiring in the room that was to house the CRL's new multimedia lab, and in implementing the building's connection to the campus network. By the time the work was done and the Multimedia Lab actually came on-line in the Fall of 1993, the institutional structure to which the CRL belonged had changed substantially.

In 1990 and '91, the English Department was caught up in a bitter struggle over proposed changes in the syllabus for the first-year composition coursc, E 306, a University-wide requirement; the dispute was widely reported in the press, where it became entangled in the national argument over "political correctness" that surrounded the Persian Gulf War. In September 1992, then-Dean Robert King of the College of Liberal Arts announced in a memorandum to English faculty that a new Division of Rhetoric and Composition would begin operating independently of the English Department on June 1, 1993.

The Division of Rhetoric and Composition would be responsible for all undergraduate writing instruction formerly under the administrative purview of the English Department. This included the required first-semester writing course, E 306, as well as a number of intermediate and advanced writing courses and courses in the history and theory of rhetoric.

The graduate program in Rhetoric, which had provided the theoretical and pedagogical foundation for the CRL, would continue to be administered by the English Department. Administrative responsibility for the Computer Research Lab itself would shift to the new Rhetoric Division, whose director, Lester Faigley, took a far more active interest in instructional uses of computers than did his counterpart in the English Department. Other members of the Rhetoric faculty responded positively as well, asking "Why stop there?" when, at a planning meeting in the Fall of 1992, I proposed a goal of teaching 50 per cent of our undergraduate writing courses on line by 1999. The Lab has been renamed the Computer Writing and Research Lab to emphasize our renewed commitment to continuing innovation in computer-based writing instruction.

A New Funding Method for Instructional Computing

Two months after the Division of Rhetoric and Composition opened its doors, the University began collecting the revenue generated by a new Instructional Technology and Computing (ITAC) fee approved by the Board of Regents the previous Spring (Danielson, 1993). Each student pays a fee of $6.00 per credit hour, per semester. The substantial revenues generated by this fee (there are over 49,000 students at UT Austin) are specifically dedicated to instructional computing activities; computers used for research purposes are paid for from other sources. The University has used the money to build a new 200-station public lab in the Undergraduate Library (a second one is in the planning stages), as well as providing electronic mailboxes at no additional charge for all members of the campus community; popular Internet applications like Netscape have been widely distributed on campus. Colleges and Schools solicit instructional computing proposals from their constituent departments, and submit these proposals to a campus-wide body consisting of both faculty and students; funds are then returned to the College level for disbursement.

Effects of the ITAC Fee

The ITAC fee has made a huge difference in the campus computing environment. As of early February 1995, 52 per cent of all students at the University had established individually-funded computer accounts (that is, for services beyond the free electronic mailbox service I mentioned above). Still more impressive, 48 per cent of students in Liberal Arts have set up individually funded accounts—up from just 14 per cent in November 1993 (two months after the fee was first levied).[16]

Recent Developments in the CWRL

With funds allocated to us out of the Instructional Technology and Computing fee levied in 1993-94, we replaced the equipment we purchased in 1991 and added a third and then a fourth computer classroom; the latter are in Parlin Hall, where English Department and Rhetoric Division offices (and most classrooms) are housed. As of Fall 1997, we are teaching 44 classes per semester in our four classrooms; these run the gamut from first-semester writing to graduate seminars in Computers and Rhetoric as well as both introductory and advanced courses in literature. [17] We have also upgraded the Multimedia Lab and installed additional networked computer facilities for graduate students. These facilities support graduate students enrolling in the new Master's and Doctoral concentrations in Computers and English Studies; approved by the English Department's Graduate Studies Committee in December 1994, this Ph.D. concentration now enrolls a dozen students.

It is not for me to say what course computer-assisted language instruction will follow; the essays in this volume will tell you far more than I could. I am convinced, however, that the introduction of computers into second-language instruction will have a transforming effect, not only upon classroom practice, but also upon departmental organization and the institutional structures that support instruction. Specific effects will vary from institution to institution, depending upon local conditions and local histories: in order to understand the narrative I have presented, it is essential to understand that the work of the Computer Writing and Research Lab and my own individual work have taken place in an institutional context far more complex than I have been able to describe here. There is also a broader context of developments within the computer industry that must be taken into account as well. Five years ago, our work in the Computer Research Lab was centered almost exclusively on Daedalus and the development of network-based pedagogy for undergraduate writing instruction—meaning, by *network*, a *local area network* in which traffic was restricted to the room in which the computers were located (or, more strictly, to the specific network to which they were connected). This emphasis has changed, however, as the technologies available to us have developed. Since 1992, for example, members of the CWRL staff have been using InterChange as part of a panoply of applications including multimedia and a wide range of Internet applications such as newsgroups, electronic mail and listservs, and, more recently, the World Wide Web, to transform instruction in both literature and writing.[18] We have also hired an additional faculty member, Margaret Syverson, with expertise in Computers and Writing, who joined the Rhetoric faculty in September 1994. Meanwhile graduate students who trained in the CWRL are employed in teaching graduate students who trained in the CWRL are employed in teaching positions at a range of universities, and instructors on more than 200 campuses on three continents are using the Daedalus Integrated Writing Environment and other software for network-based instruction in English and ESL as well as other languages. We will have to wait and see how—or whether—our institutions adapt to the challenges of the new technology and the pedagogies that have begun to appear in response to it.

Notes

[1]Project QUEST continues on a much smaller scale. It is now funded, however, by Apple Computer, Inc.

[2]In the early days of Project QUEST, successful projects were often awarded additional computers to expand their scope of operation. This happened in my own case (I started with one computer, and eventually obtained six), and in Bump's case an original award of four PC's grew to a total of 38.

[3]Besides Kemp, the graduate students involved were Paul Taylor, now at Texas A & M University; Wayne Butler, now at the University of Michigan; Valerie Balester, also at Texas A & M; Kay Halasek, at Ohio State University; Nancy Peterson, at Morehead State University; and Locke Carter, currently Chief Executive Officer of the Daedalus Group, Inc.

[4]John Hayes, co-author with Linda Flower of important essays describing the writing process, is a cognitive scientist at Carnegie-Mellon University.

[5]At a 1986 conference, Kemp heard Batson speak about what he called ENFI, or Electronic Networks for Interaction, in which Batson used written messages over a computer network as a way to help deaf students whose first language was often American Sign Language develop fluency in English. By the time Kemp and Batson met, the ENFI concept had already been implemented on a number of campuses thanks to a grant Batson had received from the Annenberg-CPB project, and a software tool, Real Time Writer, had been developed. See also LeBlanc, 1993; and Taylor, 1993.

[6]Bruffee's ideas were introduced to Kemp, Taylor, Carter, et al., by fellow Rhetoric students Kay Halasek, Nancy Peterson, and Valerie Balester. Wayne Butler, with a background in English Education, also contributed importantly to the evolving collaborative theory.

[7]The Daedalus Group was incorporated in March 1988, through a combination of accidents, misunderstandings, and entrepreneurial enthusiasm, to develop a commercial product modeled on the experiments in the Computer Research Lab. Produced with computers and programming software purchased with the financial help of family and friends, the Daedalus Instructional System, or *DIScourse,* was released in 1989. I should declare at this point that I do have a financial interest in the Daedalus Group, Inc. Readers must therefore weigh my enthusiasm against the results reported in this volume and elsewhere, and against their own experiences as well.

[8]Administrators may object that such a staffing model is expensive. I would argue, however, that it is highly cost-effective precisely because it provides professional training for graduate students simultaneously with undergraduate instruction and because the discussions about teaching raise the general level of consciousness about pedagogy in the department at large. Graduate students trained in this way have tended to do better in the increasingly depressed academic job market than those without computer experience.

[9]We were still using the original complement of IBM PC's supplied by Project QUEST. The machines had been delivered in 1986, but the design itself was some seven years old. The computers were powered by 4.77MHz Intel 8088 processors, had 512K RAM and two 5.25" 360K diskette drives; each machine also had an expansion unit, a separate chassis containing a 10 megabyte hard drive.

[10]I had developed a questionnaire and mailed it to the heads of 51 English departments, making an effort to include private as well as state-supported four-year colleges and land-grant institutions as well as research universities. I received 30 responses.

[11]The computer was a CompuAdd PC AT with 1 megabyte of RAM and a 200 megabyte hard drive. CompuAdd is no longer in the PC business, and entry-level PCs ("AT" stood for "advanced technology") now come equipped with hard drives five times that size.

[12]Scanners and Optical Character Recognition (OCR) software are now widely available for less than $500. In 1989, however, prices had just come down dramatically— from $15,000 in 1988 to $7,500 or so, signalling a dramatic increase in the market for such devices. Raymond Kurzweil was the first to apply artificial intelligence techniques to the problem of converting mere images into intelligible text; his invention, the Kurzweil Reader, combining what he called Intelligent Character Recognition with synthetic speech so that it read printed pages aloud, caused tremendous excitement in the visually impaired community, which is where I learned about it. The first Kurzweil machines came on the market in the mid-1980s at prices in the $40,000 range.

[13]The distinction between "computer classroom" and "computer lab" is an extremely important one (see Papert, 1993). A computer classroom is a computer-equipped (and networked) room where students enrolled in a particular class meet on a regular basis, just as they would in a more traditional classroom; a lab is a space where people go for work that supplements classroom activity. The instructor who teaches in a computer classroom participates with the students in an ongoing and evolving relationship that includes the technology, while a teacher who sends students to do their work in a computer lab often has little knowledge of what they do there or how the equipment works. This is not, however, an argument against labs and for classrooms: both are essential components of an effective instructional computing environment.

[14]The NeXT computer now serves as the Computer Writing and Research Lab's World Wide Web server (URL=http://www.en.utexas.edu), and as a server for two important text-based learning environments: AcademICK (Interactive Center for Knowledge), a graduate-student initiative that supports a variety of pedagogical and research experiments, including a simulation of Shakespearean theater; and the OWL, or Online Writing Lab, which supports the Undergraduate Writing Center administered by the Division of Rhetoric and Composition.

[15]According to a rule-of-thumb widely accepted in the computer industry, the computational power available at any given "price point" doubles roughly every 18 to 24 months. I recently spent less for 24 Apple PowerMacintoshes than I did for the far less powerful Macintosh IIsi's I bought for the CRL in 1991.

[16]There are no figures available to show how many free mailbox accounts have been established. Instructors teaching in the CWRL's computer classrooms now routinely require students to set up e-mail accounts, however, and I am personally aware of at least 20 faculty members, both in English or Rhetoric and in other departments, who conduct a great deal of course-related business via electronic mail. Dozens of classes now have their own Usenet newsgroups, and dozens more have established listservs and other automated discussion lists to support their work and facilitate student-student and student-instructor communication outside class hours.

[17]Just yesterday, I received the list of instructors requesting computer-assisted classes. For the first time, the number of requests exceeds our capacity: we have received 56 requests for 35 slots.

[18]The World Wide Web is developing at an astounding, almost terrifying rate. In November 1994, for instance, the Lycos Web Search Engine at Carnegie-Mellon University indexed 862,858 documents on the World Wide Web; as of February 15, 1995—not quite three months later—the index registered 1,754,942 documents, a nearly 100 per cent increase. A recent estimate is that the number of documents on the World Wide Web is now doubling approximately every 53 days.

References

Batson, T. (1988). The ENFI project: A network-based approach to writing instruction. *Academic Computing, 2* (5), 32.

Batson, T. (1993). The origins of ENFI. In B.C. Bruce, J.K. Peyton, & T. Batson, Eds. *Network-based classrooms: Promises and realities* (pp. 87-112). Cambridge: Cambridge UP.

Berlin, J. A. (1987). *Rhetoric and reality: Writing instruction in American colleges, 1980-1985.* Carbondale, IL: Southern Illinois UP.

Bolter, J. D. (1984). *Turing's man: Computers and western culture.* Chapel Hill, NC: North Carolina UP.

Bruffee, K. A. (1984). *A short course in writing: Practical rhetoric for teaching composition through collaborative learning.* Glendale, CA: Scott, Foresman.

Burns, H. L. (1979). *Stimulating rhetorical invention in English composition through computer-assisted instruction.* Unpublished Ph.D. dissertation, University of Texas, Austin.

Butler, W. M. (1992). *The social construction of knowledge in an electronic discourse community.* Unpublished Ph.D. dissertation, University of Texas, Austin.

Danielson, W. (1993). *Report of the President's Ad Hoc Committee on Information Technology: A recommendation concerning information age technology in the educational process at the University of Texas at Austin.* Austin, Texas: University of Texas at Austin, Ad Hoc Committee on Information Technology.

Emig, J. (1971). *The composing processes of twelfth graders.* Urbana, IL: National Council of Teachers of English.

Flower, L., & J. R. Hayes. (1980). The cognition of discovery: Defining a rhetorical problem. *College Composition and Communication, 31,* 21-32.

Flower, L., & J. R. Hayes. (1981). A cognitive process theory of writing. *College Composition and Communication, 32* (4), 365-387.

Hairston, M. (1982). The winds of change: Thomas Kuhn and the revolution in the teaching of writing. *College Composition and Communication, 33,* 76-82.

LeBlanc, P. A. (1993). *Writing teachers writing software.* Urbana, IL: National Council of Teachers of English.

Papert, S. (1993). *The children's machine: Rethinking school in the age of the computer.* New York: Basic Books.

Slatin, J. M. (1992). Is there a class in this text? Creating knowledge in the electronic classroom. In E. Barret (Ed.), *Sociomedia: Multimedia, hypermedia, and the social construction of knowledge* (pp. 27-51). Cambridge, MA: MIT Press.

Sproull, L., & S. Kiesler. (1991). *Connections: New ways of working in the networked organization.* Cambridge, MA: MIT Press.

Taylor, P. H. (1993). *Computer conferencing and chaos: A study in fractal discourse.* Unpublished Ph.D. dissertation, University of Texas, Austin.

Turkle, S. (1992). Paradoxical reactions and powerful ideas: Educational computing in a Department of Physics. In E. Barrett (Ed.), *Sociomedia: Multimedia, hypermedia, and the social construction of knowledge* (pp. 547-578). Cambridge, MA: MIT Press.

Zuboff, S. (1988). *In the age of the smart machine: The future of work and power.* New York: Basic Books.

Section II

Case Studies: Changing Writing Behavior

The three essays in this section, by Sullivan, Chun, and Markley, document how the use of technology can actually change writing behaviors in target groups. Each of the groups is unfamiliar to some degree with linguistic norms of the standard language they wish to use. In Sullivan's and Markley's classes, that unfamiliarity is culturally-based. Many of Sullivan's American students express alienation from the standard culture because of personal experience as members of a minority group. Markley's largely Asian-born students reflect their educational training which conditions them to be reticent in the classroom, a tendency particularly characteristic for Asian women in classes taught by men. Chun's students of elementary German share sociolinguistic norms but lack the linguistic proficiency with which to articulate them. The response patterns of these three audiences illustrate how teachers can use the InterChange experience to encourage and access both linguistic and sociolinguistic performance across diverse student groups.

Sullivan explores the way networking affects a multi-ethnic English writing class. By analyzing transcripts of the class, she characterizes shifts in linguistic output that are attributable to the computer-assisted environment. Her work suggests that the distinctive options for structuring communication tasks on a network foster students' development socially and intellectually as well as linguistically. She looks at the direction or addressee of messages in terms of student response patterns: Entries supporting, challenging, elaborating, or commenting on the observations of others. In assessing these entries, Sullivan demonstrates how the network encourages students to focus on the specific language skills necessary to dissent, collaborate, negotiate, and assert themselves in a way that particularly facilitates minority students' access to the mainstream academic culture.

Offering a parallel study of a beginning foreign-language classroom, Chun's conclusions mirror Sullivan's, while expanding on their implications for specific types of language acquisition on a network. Further, she explores data among the same students enrolled in a two semester sequence. Chun's analysis reveals that the networked classroom offers students early practice in sociolinguistic, discourse management, and strategic capacities that too often are lacking in the early stages of a foreign language classroom, and that are part of the definition of proficiency in foreign language pedagogy. By analyzing class transcripts, Chun confirms that students are actively practicing taking the initiative, taking turns, giving feedback, and expressing their attitudes, even when they have comparatively restricted linguistic capacities.

Importantly, her year-long scope enables her to trace development of sentence structures and interactional strategies. Chun's results indicate that higher-order communication situations are fostered and practiced in a networked classroom. While no control groups can substantiate this assumption, most research on student participation corroborates Chun's suspicion that, even at the initial stages of foreign language learning, students in a networked classroom have more opportunities for higher-order communication than is common in most oral classrooms. Findings cited by Markley on the relationship between teacher-talk and student participation modes in teacher-fronted classes would seem to support these inferences.

Presenting data from a situation where the use of a CACD does not yield expected results, Markley's chapter analyzes session transcripts from two parallel English composition classes in order to suggest how gender and ethnic background of students will require a different pedagogy from teachers, if the CACD environment's advantages are to be upheld.

Jaeglin's findings (section 3) indicate that these experiences are valuable to most students regardless of the language or the language level queried. Chun and Markley's chapters, both of which compare facets of performance between groups, conclude that teachers must be sensitive to individual classes' different planning and classroom management needs. Ethnic and gender distribution may call for changes within levels. Between levels, the style of cognitive and linguistic tasks must be monitored.

Developing Critical Reading and Writing Skills: Empowering Minority Students in a Networked Computer Classroom

Nancy Sullivan

The Computer-Assisted Writing Course

This chapter describes how a computer-assisted course helps minority students develop a discourse community within their English composition class and, at the same time, helps them affirm the communicative value of non-standard and standard dialects. After briefly addressing the problems faced by minority students in predominantly Anglo institutions, I will analyze the participatory patterns and speech acts engaged in during a networking class in which most participants represented ethnic minorities. My goal is to illustrate how computer exchanges can promote the self-esteem of minority students and build a discourse community among "speakers" whose language and reactive patterns are truly multicultural. Finally, I suggest why such exchanges are so successful in helping minority students to communicate and acknowledge each others' cultural messages, the sociolinguistics embedded in both standard and non-standard dialects.

The Minority Dilemma

At the university level, African-Americans and Hispanics sit in classrooms dominated by Anglo professors and Anglo students. For many African-Americans and Hispanics, the university experience represents their first daily contact with a predominantly White milieu. Unprepared for their resultant cultural dislocation, many minority students experience a drop in self-esteem. They view themselves as outsiders among linguistically and socially defined in-groups. Understandably, low performance expectations and negative attitudes result. Social scientists report that African-Americans in the university do not ask for help because they are afraid of confirming negative beliefs about their scholastic abilities (Mitchell, 1990).

Compounding these problems, teachers and administrators frequently stereotype minority students on the basis of their non-standard speech.

Indeed, from early childhood, many minority school children have often been considered cognitively deficient. Understandably, these students internalize repeated negative messages about their abilities (Mitchell, 1990). Thus the messages often become self-fulfilling prophecies (Brophy, 1983; Brophy & Good, 1974; Rist, 1970).

Nonstandard English

The extent to which the language and culture of minority students are incorporated into their education seems to correspond significantly with academic success (Bourdieu & Passeron, 1979; Campos & Keating, 1984; Cummins, 1983; Rosier & Holm, 1980). The improvement of writing skills in standard English[1] and the development of strong critical thinking skills are general goals that composition teachers have for their pupils. Enabling a positive identification of students with an environment which generally has dominant-culture goals is becoming another significant objective, especially for teachers whose classes are increasingly multicultural.

One way to enable minority students is to reduce teacher talk. Another way is to provide topics for discussion which focus on language issues which have impacted their lives.[2] Readings on Black English and Bilingualism gave them opportunities to discuss culturally-relevant issues and provided them a forum to be the "experts" in the exchanges, thereby increasing self-esteem.

Institutional Context for the Present Study

In many schools across the United States, Hispanic and African-American students are particularly affected by such stereotyping. Indeed, the two groups most apt to drop out of post-secondary schools after one year of enrollment are African-Americans and Hispanics. At the University of Texas at Austin, for instance, attrition rates for African-American and Hispanic freshman are 23.1% and 21.1%, respectively, compared to 16.9% for all freshman (Office of Institutional Studies, 1992).

The minority students in the class described here had all been accepted at the University of Texas at Austin and were participating in a five-week summer session (called PREVIEW) designed to assist them in the transition from high school to the university environment. Students enrolled in PREVIEW had had computer experience, but varied in their typing abilities. They were not, however, screened for typing ability,[3] nor were they asked if they wanted to participate in a computer-assisted course. Designed particularly (but not exclusively) for African-American, Hispanic, and Mexican-American freshman with strong academic records, the PREVIEW program provides students with special orientation, group housing, and planned activities (discussion/study groups, workshops, social/

cultural activities) that share similar academic schedules.

My writing class met seven and a half hours weekly during the summer semester. All sessions were conducted in a networked computer classroom. The other PREVIEW writing classes met in oral classrooms. The class under discussion here consisted of nineteen students: seven African-Americans (one female), six Hispanics (one male), and six Anglos (one female).[4] With regard to ethnic demographics and class size, my section was representative of the group as a whole.

Profile of Interaction

A breakdown of the students' first class discussion illustrates how the electronic discussions stimulated student participation and reduced the teacher's dominance. In all, 181 individual messages were sent. Of these messages, fourteen stemmed from the instructor: one introductory message, six responses to individual student's remarks, and seven general remarks. In other words, nineteen students sent 167 messages of varying lengths (from one to eight lines) during this session. Fourteen of these messages were student to the instructor, and 107 were student to student.

The students asked questions as well as responding to and expanding upon topics. In that first hour, twenty-three questions were asked, with eight directed to the class as a whole and fifteen sent from student to student, usually asking for clarification of an earlier remark.

For the entire electronic discussion, the instructor's remarks comprised only seven percent (7%) of the total discussion in the computer conference. The students accounted for ninety-three percent (93%) of the exchanges in which all nineteen participated in the approximately forty-five minute discussion. The least number of messages sent by an individual student was four, and the most was seventeen. The average number per student was 8.35 messages.

Analysis of an electronic discussion during the final week of class reveals a similar distribution: out of 151 messages, fourteen were sent by the instructor (10.7%). Of these, four were general questions meant to get the discussion started, four were responses to specific student's statements, and three were general statements offering background information about the author of the article. Here too, students produced over ninety percent of the exchanges. The following graphic demonstrates the consistent preponderance of student interaction.

FIGURE 1. NUMBER OF MESSAGES SENT DURING 40-MINUTE INTERCHANGE SESSIONS

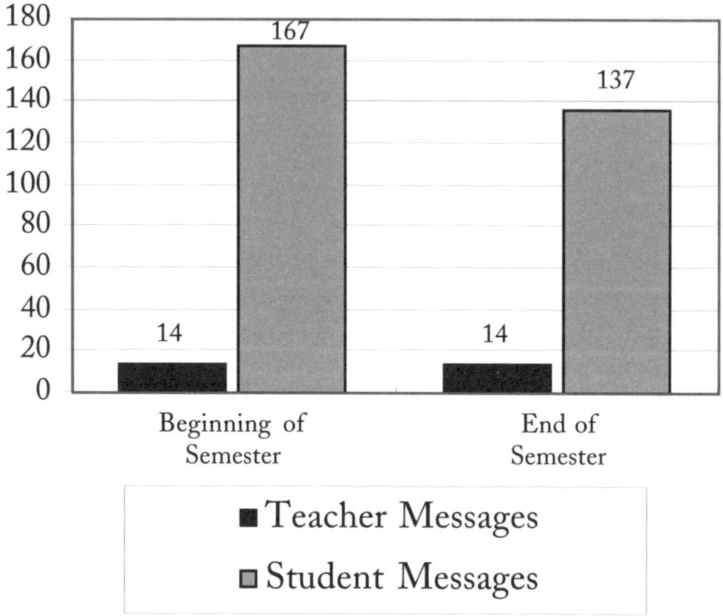

Interaction Frequency—Comparing Electronic with Oral Classrooms

The foregoing data is the more striking in view of the extant studies on verbal exchanges in traditional classrooms. In one review of teacher-talk, it was reported that exchanges in oral classrooms are initiated by the teacher eighty-one percent of the time. Out of 590 teacher-student sequences, 480 were initiated by the teacher, and 110, approximately eighteen percent, were initiated by the student (Mehan, 1979). In general, then, the research literature attributes *two-thirds of classroom utterances to the teacher*. Similarly, in studies of second-language classrooms (Chaudron, 1988; Sullivan & Pratt, 1996), sixty-five to seventy-five percent of classroom speech is attributed to the teachers. Yet, Sullivan and Pratt (1996), as well as the studies reported in this volume by Beauvois, Chun, Markley, and Kelm, found that computer-assisted classrooms reversed those percentages dramatically in favor of high student participation.

Breakdown of Interaction by Ethnicity

An examination of the electronic interactions by ethnic group reveals a pattern of progressive equalization through the semester. Figure 2 compares the mean number of turns for each ethnic group in early- and late-semester electronic InterChanges.

FIGURE 2. MEAN NUMBER OF TURNS BY ETHNIC GROUP

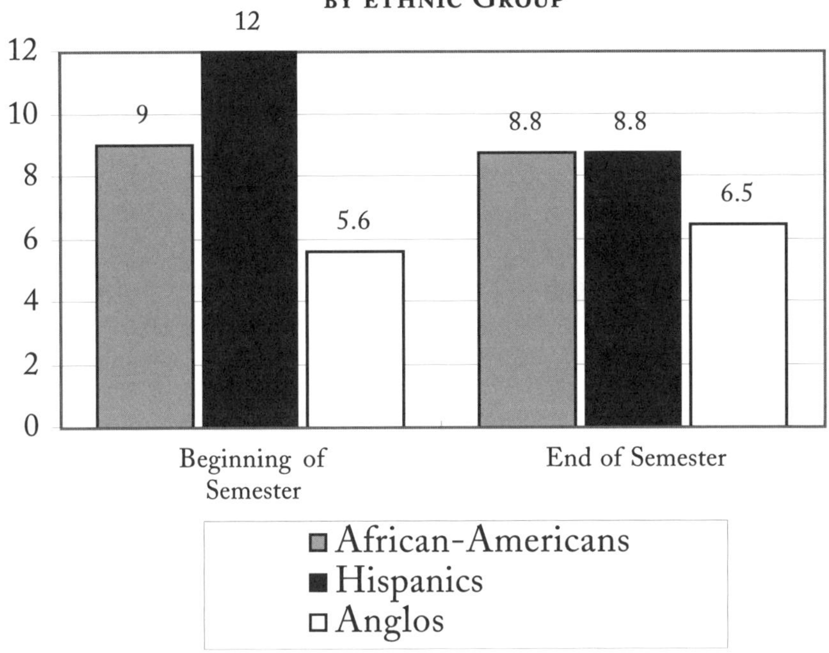

The Hispanics dominated at the beginning of the semester, while the Anglos were the least participatory. But, by the end of the semester, a more equal pattern of exchange was achieved. The Anglos increased their participation, but remained the least active of the three groups—not surprisingly, as they started the semester with a lower academic standing than the other two groups. However, not only the absolute number, but also the cooperative characteristics of the exchanges show the increasing student growth and empowerment over the course of the semester.

Interaction Styles

Collaborative exchanges. The quality of the interactions in the networking class show that these students were very aware of each other's presence. Personal exchanges on the transcript revealed classmates joking with one another, slipping in questions about personal activities, and expressing concern about one another. Viewed together, these comments convey a feeling of community and trust among the classmates. Typically, students commented about classmates who were not contributing and invited them to participate in the discussion, for example[5]:

```
Wheres Byron?

Lisa, tell Jorg

Wake up, Philip.

Chuck need to keep up.

Robert, any ideas?

David are you there. Your not even say
anything.
```

Almost invariably, such notice of nonparticipation drew a response from the individual named.

Students counted on each other for feedback on their compositions. Praise and constructive criticism were common. On balance, personal exchanges in the electronic classroom community showed largely supportive behavior.

Other roles were also developed and maintained throughout the semester. Several students interacted by assuming a particular posture or classroom role. The only African-American woman in the class, Opal assumed a "mother" role for the African-American male students and would give an electronic "tongue-lashing" to anyone who she felt unduly criticized one of her "children." The observation that a text written by an African-American man got "lost towards the end" drew from Opal the protective response that follows:

```
LENA, IF HE KNEW THAT HE WAS GETTING LOST
TOWARDS THE END HE WOULDN'T HAVE DONE IT!
```

In the oral classroom, this type of exchange would have been considered disruptive behavior. But in the electronic InterChange, Opal's irritation did not disrupt discussion. She had, in fact, sent Marvin a stronger message in an earlier InterChange:

```
WHAT IS IT THAT YOU DISAGREE WITH?  THE
MESSAGE YOU SENT MADE ABSOLUTELY NO SENSE
AT ALL!  TRY AGAIN.
```

This reproach was taken in a facilitative way. After Opal's message, the point of "not getting lost" was mentioned by several students in their subsequent entries as problem common to everyone and as a hazard to watch out for.

The behaviors observed did not only occur after students had done reviews of reading. When preparing a writing assignment, small groups of students (four or five) brainstormed in conferences—a network option on the InterChange program that is designed to accommodate small group discussions. Instructions asked conferees to work closely with each other to narrow topics, suggest development strategies with which to structure their composition, and share knowledge to which their classmates might not have access. This pre-writing activity helped students by pointing out potential controversies or focus problems. For example, students warned a classmate of the possible consequences of arguing a point in a religious context: " . . . that's a good controversial subject but . . . be careful because many people are sensitive about it."

Typically, during one brainstorming session, a student reported that he was considering writing his paper on "stereotypic words associated with men and women." One student responded that the topic was rather broad, and another offered the following:

> Tom you could narrow it down by foucusing on a certain kind of pet names for instance foucus on slang names in certain [ethnic] groups. I read something about the different categories for slang names last night in the PCL [library] on the 5th floor in the p120s I beleive but don't hold me to it.

Collaborating during electronic conferences enabled students to draw out colleagues with expertise or insights about the topic due to their cultural backgrounds. During a discussion on sexist language, for example, a Hispanic female contributed that Spanish uses male/female pronouns. Her comment was followed by this question from an African-American male:

> Lena, why is it in Spanish everything has a "male" or "female" ending. How do you feel about it now after talking about all of this sexist language?

Another African-American student added a cultural perspective which, after collaborating with classmates, he eventually developed into an essay on sexist language and African-American culture:

> I think men tend to like being called a hunk, or beefcake, but some women especially in African-American society do not always like to be called a "sweet thang" and the like. Talk to me, I need feedback.

The fostering of this kind of communal ethos was apparent even in the first electronic discussion which focused on sexist language. The exchange and sharing of knowledge continued throughout the semester.

Negotiation. One of the most appealing characteristics of computer conferencing was that the students had an opportunity to negotiate, resulting in development of communication and problem-solving skills. These activities were represented consistently in the computer transcripts. For example, students frequently negotiated by asking for clarification of remarks. In the first computer conference discussion of the class, this opinion was sent: "I agree with alot of the topic discuss in Male/Female speech." Such a general response is typical of students who, especially at the beginning of the semester, are too unsure of themselves to make any commitments. Another student directed the following question to Marvin, the reluctant student we encountered above:

> . . . IF YOU AGREE ALOT WITH THE TOPIC THEN WHAT DONT YOU AGREE WITH. IS THERE A POINT THAT BOTHERS YOU OR YOU YHINK IS IRRELEVENT TO THE MALE/FEMALE LANGUAGE.

This comment represents a sophisticated negotiated invitation: "tell us what you think is important or not important about the differences between male and female languages."

Moreover, the non-standard English in which the comment is framed does not obscure the efficacy of the negotiation in question. For the addressee, also a non-standard speaker, the rhetorical force of a negotiation is probably greater for having been couched in non-standard form. Possibly for this reason, students incorporate the positive negotiating styles in messages they receive from peers into their own subsequent verbalizations about others. Near the end of the semester, Marvin, who had earlier been criticized because he often "agreed a lot," informed a classmate that while he liked her review, it had problems with lack of clarity.

Students also negotiated about the intent of their observations, often rephrasing and clarifying assertions in response to disagreement. The following extended discourse took place during the discussion of a reading that focused on the terms "African-American" and "White" and the connotations of each (African-American-evil / White-good). It illustrates the negotiating moves in a relatively complex sequence that extends beyond what is typically found in an oral classroom, but which was reasonably frequent on the network. To pinpoint this distinction, the sequences in the speech acts are noted in brackets following each example:

> *Maria* (Hispanic female): I think Jaime is right, when they are defining those terms they aren't talking about PEOPLE. That's why I think that given the chance, people will find a way to turn nothing into something. [*an opinion*]

Opal (African-American female): NO MARIA THEY AREN'T TALKING ABOUT "PEOPLE." BUT SADLY ENOUGH, COLOR IS THE WAY THAT PEOPLE ARE REFERRED TO; THEREFORE, I DON'T AGREE WITH THE FACT THAT YOU THINK THEY ARE MAKING SOMETHING OUT OF NOTHING [*argued rejection of opinion*]

Maria (Hispanic female): Opal, do you really think people think of you by negative connotations to a color? Are all white people pure and wonderful? HA!!! [*challenge to the belief systems driving the rejection of the opinion*]

Lena (Hispanic female): Maria are you saying that the author was over emphasizing the importance of these two wor[d]s? [*inquiry designed to focus discussion on issues rather than affect*]

Maria (Hispanic female): Lena- no- I'm just saying that I don't think people think of negative connotations to the word African-American every time they speak. [*clarification of the basis for the challenge to Opal*]

Maria held to her viewpoint that people should not be so easily offended or sensitive. Typically for all students engaging in such exchanges, in the process of clarifying and defending her intent, Maria's English statements became progressively more succinct, sophisticated, and clear.

By means of such negotiations, then, two objectives are served. Issues are clarified, and with such clarifications, student language usage tends to improve. The students are learning to be expressive in the standard language, or, said another way, they begin to recognize both *that* they are negotiating in a particular way and *how* to express that negotiation clearly. Also important is that it is students (and those of all ethnic groups), not the instructor, who prod classmates into making these more precise statements in support of their arguments.

Dissent. As already indicated, even dissent or arguments become linguistic issues instead of affective ones for students on the network. Face-to-face interaction, especially between teacher and student, is often intimidating for students, which often inhibits dissent (see Swaffar, this volume). Consequently, voicing an opposing argument to that of the teacher is difficult for a majority of students. However, most students can more freely give voice to dissent in front of a computer because computers are non-confrontational. Therefore, a computer screen and a keyboard can be considered a more risk-free environment than the normally interrogatory classroom.

In the class under discussion, dissent on computer exchanges was not always characterized by a reasoned meeting of the minds. Sometimes it resulted in a strident response, followed by a refusal to engage. In the discussion on African-American English, for example, one Hispanic female asked whether African-American English should be considered a separate language, since one article described it as having its own form and structure. Opal, an African-American, apparently took offense at this comment and gave the following reply:

> . . . SO WHAT YOU ARE SAYING IS, THAT IF PEOPLE WHO SPEAK AFRICAN-AMERICAN ENGLISH CANNOT DROP THEIR DIALECT LIKE A DIME AND PICK UP "THE WHITE MAN'S LANGUAGE" THAT IT SHOULD BE CONSIDERED A SEPARATE LANGUAGE. MAYBE IT'S ME, BUT THAT IS THE MESSAGE THAT YOU SEEM TO BE SENDING.

The Hispanic student who asked the question chose not to reply—an option barely noticed in a classroom exchange where entries of all kinds appear in chronological sequence, not isolated out as particular exchanges that call for a particular kind of closure. In an oral classroom, such a response would likely have led to confrontation or humiliation. The Hispanic student would have been put on the spot and would have had to make some sort of verbal (or non-verbal) reply to this question. In contrast, the computer format allows participants to pursue or drop issues without confrontation—or to return to them later when they can deal with the issue instead of the affect. As a result, fear of consequences is far less a factor in deciding to disagree than is characteristically the situation in a classroom.

Instead, the students in this class were able to investigate the "role that controversy and intellectual divergence play in learning and thinking" (Cooper & Selfe, 1990, p. 849). This is a crucial element in their empowerment as writers and speakers. When students are provided with a forum to express their ideas and consciously take part in the intellectual process of critical thinking, they are also being provided experience and practice in communicating and persuading.

One striking example of dissent that would probably not have occurred in an oral classroom took place during a week of discussions on bilingual education and the English Only movement. Students were aware that I, their instructor, was in favor of bilingualism. In response to several positive assertions, one Hispanic female countered:

"All I'm say is that bilingual Education is detrimental to society. It does not place enough importance on English as a means for a successful life." Another Hispanic female added:

"People don't understand that it [adoption of English as the official language] is for the good of the whole."

These students were thus not only opposing the opinions of the teacher, they were also articulating views based on experiences not shared by most other students in the group. Many of these students had experienced bilingual education programs and found them severely lacking. They have lived in communities where Spanish is the primary language for communication, and they have witnessed what happens socially and economically to those who do not speak English. In the course of the subsequent discussion of these opinions, these students contributed unique expertise and insights. Moreover, their dissent convinced several African-American students whose comments suggested that they supported the position of their Hispanic classmates over that of the teacher.

Thoughtful dissent from purported authority was not restricted to peers and teachers, however. In the course of exchanges, students also questioned textual assertions. For example, students were sensitive to George Will's flag-waving strategy for promoting his ideas about the English language. They rejected it in statements such as the following:

> *Gregory* (African-American male): Everyone, don't be fooled by Will's use of sentimentality and emotions in the essay. It's natural to get a warm feeling in your heart when someone talks about cute, little puppy dogs, religion, your family, or even being patriotic to your country. Will wants you to feel that way towards English, but to put this language above all others is just a way to make other languages subcomb to the ruling classes language.

Such challenges to textual authority, uncharacteristic in oral classrooms, occurred during every networking session, which again suggests that the students actively engaged in their roles as critics and writers.

Conclusions and Implications

As the transcripts above document, the computer-assisted classroom encourages collaborative learning and social interaction. Several more specific results are worth individual comment, since they appear to be fostered by a networking environment.

The transcripts of the class discussed above document the increased quantity of linguistic production for groups of students who historically have demonstrated low participation in the traditional classroom. While quantity of engagement is significant in itself, the results presented here also allow some preliminary speculations about qualitative differences in the language use produced. On an absolute scale of correctness, to be sure, many of the exchanges offered suffer from grammatical and spelling defects. However, as noted, as the students gained confidence and as they realized the specific kinds of interaction that the network facilitated, their willingness to participate, fostered by networking, enabled them to practice rhetorical strategies leading to effective, if not always formally accurate, communication.

Thus the "correctness" issue itself would be the wrong focus for an analysis of results. The real benefit for this particular group of students was that they were able to define themselves by their communicative skills in a particular type of discussion where value was not located in prior language abilities or "background" (in either a negative or positive sense), but in their ability to use language to clarify issues at hand.

The case of Opal (an African-American female) who wrote all in capital letters is instructive at this point, for it is a prototype for how students were able to establish roles and distinct voices in this classroom. Opal, an aggressive, articulate student, was typing everything in caps by the second computer conference. Yet as her care in giving both praise and blame to her classmates demonstrates, she was not offensive, just outspoken. I told her that she even managed to shout at people electronically during the computer conference (partially through her use of caps). Opal's use of capital letters set her comments off visually on the screen, just as she would have preferred her verbal utterances to be highlighted. However, Opal was not able to dominate the discussion—the networking classroom makes dominance through force of personality difficult. Instead, Opal was integrated into the classroom, while she was forced to monitor her own intelligibility and effectiveness in strictly communicative terms.

The computer transcripts also testify that students developed writing and thinking skills in tandem. For example, Marvin, referred to above, had the lowest writing skills of the class, as traditionally defined. In the beginning of the semester, he contributed only three percent of the total discussion. By the end of the semester he had more than doubled that to seven percent, which argues for his engagement and learning in quantitative terms. Yet there was a qualitative shift in his contributions as well, reflecting a development in his sense of linguistic strategy and communication—a development that arguably is as important as the quantity and general linguistic correctness of his work. Even though Marvin entered his messages late in the discussion (usually after everyone else had sent at least two messages), he would eventually join in. Yet later in each session, Marvin's contributions became more than just agreements; he began to provide concise arguments substantiated by appropriate supporting statements. He thus did not suddenly become loquacious, but he learned to capitalize on his role in each exchange, which added both length and substance to his contributions.

Through the use of the electronic medium, the students in this class were thus able to become increasingly sensitive to the written medium of communication as it related to their personal needs and wants. They developed strong written discourse strategies through interacting, collaborating, and negotiating meaning electronically. Moreover, it seems that students became sensitive to options for verbal expression: they were aware when they were negotiating, collaborating, dissenting, and asserting themselves—complicated acts of communication—in a way that is much less likely to occur in the oral classroom. In oral classrooms, group work too easily loses focus, or becomes a situation for personalities to dominate. In the electronic classroom (even beyond the types of discussions used as the examples here), different heuristic programs for invention and revision that allow various combinations of small groups give students clearly defined tasks by setting productive group work in distinct communication environments (persuading, brainstorming, and the like). The electronic programs thus create various (and often discrete) public forums for student contributions, thereby encouraging students to take responsibility for those contributions, both affectively and in terms of communication tasks. As the above transcripts indicate, progressively more sophisticated and varied argumentation on issues was fostered by the extensive discourse options available in the computer-assisted classroom.

Finally, through use of the computer environment, this class was able to turn potentially contentious discussions focusing on social and cultural issues into opportunities that stimulated self-exploration and expression. The electronic forum provided the platform from which all students could be heard and from which they could exercise the power of language.

Notes

[1]The term "standard English" here is used as defined in the *Longman Dictionary of Language Teaching and Applied Linguistics* (1992): "the variety of a language which has the highest status in a community of nation and which is usually based on the speech and writing of educated native speakers of the language" (351).

[2]Each of the five weeks had a topic focusing on a language-related issue: Gender and Speech, African-American English, Bilingualism, Taboo Language, and Abusive Language. The readings were used as the basis for the discussions and writing assignments. The students read twenty-four articles during the five weeks in addition to writing one article review, three essays (one of which was outside of class with two drafts), a research paper with several drafts, and a final in-class essay. The readings were used as the basis for the writing assignments and the research paper was the further development of one of their previous papers. With only five weeks to do a semester's work, the students worked intensively throughout the entire academic period.

At the beginning of the course, each student signed up to write a one-page review of one of the articles (a short summary followed by a critical reaction). The students were given specific instructions on how to prepare the article review along with an example. In addition to these readings, the students received various handouts and worksheets which dealt with library research, the writing process (organization, argumentation strategies), and language (jargon, sexist language, etc.).

[3]As you will see below, the issue of typing abilities is important: some "language errors" in the transcripts are actually typing errors, since they do not recur consistently. During a discussion, such errors were not corrected if they did not detract from comprehensibility—errors were monitored in the formal writing exercises.

[4]The Anglo students were an unexpected addition to the class. They were all freshmen who had entered the university on probation because of low academic standing. They were a welcome addition as they offered another cultural perspective to the discussions.

[5]Transcripts have been reprinted from originals, but names have been changed. Deviance from standard usage such as spelling or typographical errors have, thus, been preserved.

References

Bourdieu, P., & Passeron, J. (1979). *The inheritors: French students and their relation to culture*. Chicago: University of Chicago Press.

Brophy, J. (1983). Conceptualizing student motivation. *Educational Psychologist, 18*, 200-215.

Brophy, J., & Good, T. (1974). *Teacher-student relationships: Causes and consequences*. New York: Holt, Rinehart & Winston.

Campos, J., & Keating, B. (1984). *The Carpinteria preschool program: Title VII second year evaluation report*. Washington, DC: Department of Education.

Chaudron, C. (1988). *Second language classrooms: Research on teaching and learning*. Cambridge: Cambridge University Press.

Cooper, M., & Selfe, C. (Dec. 1990). Computer conferences and learning: Authority, resistance and internally persuasive discourse. *College English, 52* (8), 847-869.

Cummins, J. (1983). *Heritage language education: A literature review*. Toronto: Ministry of Education.

Mehan, H. (1979). *Learning lessons: Social organization in the classroom*. Cambridge, MA: Harvard University Press.

Mitchell, J. (1990). Reflections of a Black social scientist: Some struggles, some doubts, some hopes. In N.M. Hildage, S.L. Dowell, & E.V. Siddle, eds., *Facing racism in education*, pp. 118-134. Cambridge, MA: Harvard Educational Review, Reprint Series No. 21.

Office of Institutional Studies, University of Texas at Austin (1992). *Undergraduate student flow by ethnicity and foreign status*. Austin, TX: University of Texas.

Rist, R.C. (1970). Students' social class and teacher expectations: The self-fulfilling prophecy in ghetto education. *Harvard Educational Review, 40*, 411-451.

Rosier, P., & Holm, W. (1980). *The Rock Point experience: A longitudinal study of a Navajo school*. Washington, DC: Center for Applied Linguistics.

Sullivan, N., & Pratt, E. (1996). A comparative study of two ESL writing environments: A computer-assisted classroom and a traditional oral classroom. *System, 29*(4), 491-501.

Using Computer-Assisted Class Discussion to Facilitate the Acquisition of Interactive Competence

Dorothy M. Chun

I. Introduction

One of the foremost advantages of using computers for any pedagogical purpose is its purported interactive capability. However, without artificial intelligence (AI), real communicative interaction between user and computer is limited at present. What computers can facilitate, though, is human interaction among people in the same room as well as continents apart. For language learners in particular, computer networks and electronic mail provide students with opportunities for authentic communication with native speakers of the target language.[1] Local area networks (LANs) have been used in intermediate and advanced foreign language and English as a Second Language (ESL) classes, as well as in English literature or composition courses for native English speakers, with great success.[2] Indeed, the availability and use of current technologies that support computer-assisted language learning (CALL) and computer-mediated communication (CMC) raise the critical question of whether or not there is a paradigm shift in how languages are taught and learned (cf. Kaiser, 1997).

While much of the previous research focuses on the use of networking to improve writing and the thought processes involved in writing, this chapter suggests that networking can be used successfully and effectively with beginning language learners to increase their spoken and written communicative language proficiency (CLP).[3] Specifically, the main thesis is that Computer-Assisted Class Discussion (CACD) provides learners with the opportunity to generate and initiate different kinds of discourse, which in turn enhances their ability to express a greater variety of *functions*

A version of this article appeared in *System* 4(4) (1996) and is being reprinted here with permission of Elsevier Press.

in different *contexts* as well as to play a greater role in managing the discourse. They feel freer to address questions to anyone or everyone in the class, to query the teacher from time to time, to suggest new topics or steer the discussion towards things they are interested in, to request more information or confirmation of something said by someone else, or to express thoughts or opinions that have not been explicitly solicited.

Data were collected over a two-semester period from first-year German students using a real-time networking program on the Macintosh. The written discourse produced in fourteen sessions of CACD was analyzed with regard to the following characteristics: 1) the number and length of turns or entries each student makes in a CACD session, 2) the quality of each entry, in terms of syntactic complexity (e.g., which syntactic forms are used to express particular speech acts) and 3) the type and number of different discourse structures (e.g., responses to questions, questions asked of fellow students, initiation of a new topic, circumlocutions or paraphrases, negotiation of meaning). As Swaffar (1992) suggests, these data show that when using a network "students engage in communicative and cognitive assessment of ideas, as well as . . . in rhetorical and morphosyntactic practice."[4] In addition, they are directly and actively involved in the management of the discourse or interaction.

II. Previous Research

This section reviews briefly the major goals of the communicative competence and proficiency movements (Subsection A), with particular focus on the non-grammatical aspects of language. For example, *sociolinguistic* and *interactive* competence, which proficient speakers must acquire or learn and for which CACD provides an ideal context, includes the ability to perform different speech acts and to negotiate meaning. In addition, I give a short overview of research to date on the use of networked computers for teaching writing (Subsection B).

A. Teaching Interactive Competence/Proficiency

This chapter is concerned primarily with how CACD helps to develop sociolinguistic, discourse and strategic competence in foreign language learners as described in both the communicative competence and proficiency movements.[5] CACD allows learners greater freedom to generate and practice a variety of functions in different contexts of the type outlined in the *ACTFL Proficiency Guidelines*[6] and extended or revised models of proficiency (e.g., Kramsch's (1983, 1986) proposals for interactional competence). Kramsch (1983) suggests that communicative competence must include the ability to express, interpret and negotiate meanings and advocates that students be given opportunities in the classroom to go beyond traditional teacher-centered, teacher-initiated discourse in which students primarily answer questions. In striving for as natural a communicative situation as possible, students must be given the chance to manage classroom discourse and interact with both the instructor and fellow students through turn-taking, expanding on topics, giving feedback to speakers, capturing attention, steering or avoiding topics, and starting and ending conversations. Byrnes (1987, pp. 301-302) also advocates a greater emphasis on the learner, on speech as a process, and on the negotiative and interactive process of speaking. Current research is broadening the scope of competence to include sociocultural competence as well (cf. Herring, 1996; Kramsch, 1995).

Note that the *ACTFL Proficiency Guidelines* provide separate criteria for the different skills. For example, an "intermediate" level *speaker* is described as able to ask and answer questions, initiate, sustain, and close basic communicative tasks with basic conversational strategies, narrate and describe simply in connected discourse, but at times must resort to unexpected circumlocution. In the descriptions of *writing* proficiency, for the same "intermediate" level, learners are expected to meet most practical writing needs (e.g., writing letters, taking notes, creating statements or questions, describing and narrating in paragraphs).[7] Data from this study will be analyzed below with regard to these criteria.

B. Computers and Teaching Writing

Raimes (1992, p. v) states that reading, thinking, talking, and writing about a subject are all essential parts of the writing process and that "for second-language students, these activities are especially valuable, as they provide many opportunities for communication in the new language." She adds that both the process of revising what one has written and getting feedback from readers are also essential. To varying degrees, these activities are all possible with computer networking and thus, networks may be an effective tool for teaching writing.[8]

There are two main types of networks: 1) the Internet, which is internationally accessible and allows users to share information via electronic mail, bulletin boards, and discussion lists and 2) Local Area Networks (LANs), which link computers in an office, a department, or a laboratory to each other. Examples of previous research with both of these types of networks follows.

Cononelos and Oliva (1992) used an electronic bulletin board called *NEWS* on the Internet network with an advanced Italian-language course focusing on the society and culture of Italy. They believe that "computer networks hold the greatest promise for language teachers seeking interactive media." Their students all believed that their writing improved as a result of having communicated through the network. The instructors felt that the feedback gained by the students from responses of native speakers who are not language teachers, but share with the students a common area of interest, was an important factor in improving the students' writing. "Communicating through *NEWS* allows for an ongoing conversation to develop between many participants. Student work not only generates counter-responses directed to them but also sparks dialogue between respondents. This makes students co-creators of text generated by parties authentically interested in the subjects they have chosen" and makes composition classes more learner-centered.

Warschauer's (1995a) description of using e-mail for teaching English can easily be applied to the teaching of foreign languages, and Kern (1996) reported on using e-mail exchanges to explore personal histories in two cultures. Warschauer (1995b) listed a multitude of projects that make use of both the Internet as well as LANs. The collection of papers in Warschauer (1996b) also attest to the plethora of telecollaborative work in foreign language teaching.

Bump (1990) showed that use of a LAN with computer-assisted class discussion (CACD) software was effective in English courses.[9] Some of the advantages of CACD found in his and other studies include intense collaboration among students and between students and teacher, increased student participation, particularly of minorities and women, decentralization of the instructor's role and therefore more learner-centered, more "honest" communication (e.g. more self-disclosure, expression of emotion), and improved thinking and creativity. Disadvantages include technostress or technophobia, slow speed as compared with speaking, insufficient voice communication, loss of coherence in discussion of a topic, loss of teacher control, too direct or confrontational a style (e.g., profanity, negative affect, use of capitalization and exclamation points), and the problem of not being able to see the forest for the trees.

At the time the current study was conducted (1991-92), there was little published research on CACD in foreign language instruction, either in terms of advantages and disadvantages, or in particular, with regard to the types of utterances or sentences that learners produce in certain discourse contexts to perform a variety of discourse functions.[10] One of my central hypotheses was that using CACD would provide students with the opportunity to generate and initiate different kinds of discourse structures or speech acts. Students would feel freer to ask questions about things they are interested in, to address questions to different members of the class, including the teacher, to change the subject at their leisure and discretion, to expand on topics or abandon topics, to express thoughts or opinions (particularly negative ones) that they might not in an oral discussion, and in general, to take a more active role in discourse management.

In a normal classroom, a common vehicle to provide opportunities for learner-centered oral discourse to develop the above-mentioned competence is small-group activity or pair work. However, it is all too common that students revert to their native language once the teacher is no longer within earshot. An advantage of CACD is that the entire class, as well as the teacher, reads everything everyone else writes, and students might thus feel more compelled to use only the target language. In addition, since there is no time pressure, they might take the time and effort to express themselves in the target language rather than take the easy way out by using their native language to say something complicated. As an added benefit of CACD, the fact that students have unlimited time to formulate their comments allows them to describe, narrate, and expand on topics much more freely and easily than in any type of oral situation where they feel more of a sense of immediacy to respond or say something.

III. Data: Longitudinal Study of First-Year German Students

Data were collected over two semesters from first- and second-semester German classes taught by the author. In both semesters it was the only "honors" section being offered; thus, there was overlap in the student population. In the first semester (Fall 1991), fourteen students were enrolled, eight women and six men. In the second semester (Spring 1992), eight of the original fourteen students were enrolled, four women and four men, and a ninth student, a male, also joined the group. During the first semester, only five computer networking sessions were conducted during the latter half of the semester (after the students had learned enough rudimentary vocabulary and grammar to conduct a sustained conversation), and these sessions lasted for approximately 15-20 minutes each. During the second semester, nine sessions were conducted for periods varying between 20-45 minutes, averaging approximately 25 minutes each.

The software used was the *InterChange* function of the *Daedalus Integrated Writing Environment* software, which allows for real-time, synchronous Computer-Assisted Classroom Discussion (CACD) on a Local Area Network (LAN). Students were given oral instructions about the topic(s) of discussion before going to the computer lab, and the questions were repeated in writing as one of the first entries from the instructor at the beginning of each computer discussion. Topics for discussion ranged from weekend activities to complaints from parents about young people today, from travel experiences abroad to whether or not condom machines should be installed on campus. Discussions were saved verbatim on the computer, and transcripts of the entire session were printed, greatly facilitating analysis of the data.

From the transcripts, various features about the quantity and quality of the language used in the discussions were examined: 1) the number and length of turns or entries by each student, 2) the syntactic or grammatical complexity of the entries, and 3) the type and number of different discourse structures by individual students and, in some cases, by students according to gender. The first two types of features are discussed briefly in Subsection A below and the third type in more detail in Subsection B.

A. General Characteristics of Turns

Since the focus of this discussion is the way students use language to express communicative functions, I will only summarize the data with regard to number and length of turns by each student and the syntactic complexity of each entry (i.e., number of simple and complex sentences and types of syntactic forms which are used to express particular speech acts).

In general, the data from these particular groups of students show that during a typical 20-25 minute session, the average number of entries made by individual students ranged from a low of 2.8 to a high of 17.8 (see Appendix 1). It is important to note here that length of entries was left completely up to the students and ranged from simple one-sentence entries to paragraph-length entries with several complex sentences. For purposes of this chapter, these differences were noted subjectively but MLU (mean length of utterance), for example, was not calculated for each individual student. What was evident was that individuals had different "styles" of discussing. At one end of the spectrum were those who expressed one idea at a time with simple grammatical structures, and at the other end were those who expressed more complete thoughts in paragraphs, with several sentences and often with greater syntactic complexity as well. Due to the small size of the sample, generalizations cannot be made with regard to style, gender, personality or otherwise.

Of possible interest because it counters previous research is that in this group of students, several of the quieter, shyer ones were indeed the most "prolific" in the computer discussions. However, unlike previous studies which found increased participation by women (cf. Bump, 1990, Markley, 1992), three of the four most active participants in my small sample were males who normally were relatively quiet in class. While they made a lot of entries, averaging 9.0, 14.1, and 17.8 entries per 20-25 minute session, two of them usually wrote relatively short entries (i.e., typically one or two sentences). The third, who averaged 9.0 entries per session wrote longer entries, usually consisting of several relatively long sentences. One could sense that they all were (and wanted to be) actively involved in the class discussion. In contrast, some of the less extroverted female students tended to make fewer entries, averaging 2.8, 4.7 and 5.8, respectively, but they generally wrote paragraph-length responses. Interestingly, the student who averaged only 5.8 (not particularly long) entries per session was by far the most sophisticated essay writer in both classes.

In terms of the syntactic complexity of entries, for the five sessions during the first semester, approximately 3 times as many simple sentences (161) were written as compound or complex (48) (see Appendix 2). In the nine sessions from the second semester, students still wrote more simple than complex sentences, but the ratio improved (399:297). In other words, for every 4 simple sentences, they wrote 3 compound or complex ones. This seems to be a favorable ratio for first-year language learners. When broken down according to gender, males generally wrote more than females (overall 519 sentences by males to 386 by females, and 363 simple sentences by males to 197 by females), but the women wrote slightly more compound or complex sentences (189) than males (156). These differences may be attributable to any number of factors (e.g., writing style, possibly gender, language aptitude, ability to write cohesively and coherently in English). Unfortunately, however, this was not the focus of my investigation.

B. *Interactive Characteristics of Turns*

I now turn to the functional features of language which are the focus of this chapter. Table 1 below summarizes selected types of functional competence set forth in two standard references.[11] My data are then presented and show that first-year German students produce a variety of written entries in CACDs which reflect many of the types of interactive utterances, listed in the table, that proficient speakers need to be capable of.

TABLE I

Selected Types of Functional and Interactive Competence

ACTFL Proficiency Guidelines (1986)*	Kramsch (1983): *Interactive Competence*
• can create with the language by combining and recombining learned elements	• can create, express, interpret and negotiate meaning
• can initiate, sustain, and close basic communicative tasks	• can take turns
• can ask and answer questions	• can open and close conversations
• can initiate and respond to simple statements	• can take the initiative, capture attention
• can narrate and describe	• can construct and expand on a topic
• hesitation and circumlocution sometimes necessary	• can elaborate on others' ideas
• minimal sociolinguistic competence: can handle everyday social encounters (greetings, leave takings, the use of polite formulas)[12]	• can show and check understanding
	• can ask for clarification
	• gives feedback to others
	• can steer or avoid topics

* Intermediate Level (1/1+)

1. Summary of Observed Characteristics

All of the students in both semesters demonstrated, to differing degrees, the ability to perform the selected functions from the *ACTFL Proficiency Guidelines* listed in Table 1 above. For example, all could create with the language (i.e., they did not simply use stock phrases or memorized constructions).[13] All of them initiated and responded to simple statements, and all, to varying extents, asked and answered questions as well as used greetings, leave takings, etc. appropriately. Those who tended to write one or two sentences at a time did not clearly demonstrate their ability to narrate or describe in detail, but many of the students wrote paragraph-length entries in which these abilities were amply in evidence. Another aspect which is difficult if not impossible to ascertain in CACD is the amount of hesitation and ensuing circumlocution. One observation that can be made is that students did not always seem to paraphrase when they didn't know a particular vocabulary item. Instead, they would simply use the English word or phrase. However, unlike with small-group or pair work, where one often hears students uttering entire sentences in English, there were

no complete English sentences in the entire corpus of 14-sessions, but rather single words in English and occasionally a phrase when the German equivalent was not known.[14]

With regard to the types of interactive competence described by Kramsch (1983, 1986) and the activities suggested by Raimes (1992), an important first observation is that virtually *all* of the questions, whether general or specific, posed by both teacher and students were answered. This indicates that students were reading everything that was produced and were processing, comprehending, and interpreting a tremendous amount of input. Turn-taking in a computer discussion is different from verbal conversations, but most of the other abilities in Kramsch's list were attested to: students took the initiative in asking questions of others and expanding on topics, either those they themselves constructed or those suggested by others, they asked for clarification and explanations when they wanted to check their understanding, and they gave feedback to others, typically in the form of agreement or continuation of the topic.

Based on the above-listed types of functional and interactive competence, tallies were made of the various kinds of sentences produced in the fourteen sessions of CACD conducted over two semesters (see Appendix 2). Specifically, sentences were classified, not by formal syntactic type, but rather by function within the discourse:

Questions and Answers

1. general questions posed by teacher to entire class
2. specific questions from teacher to individual student
3. general questions posed by students to entire class
4. specific questions from students to other students
5. replies to teacher's general and specific questions
6. replies to students' general and specific questions

Statements and Imperatives

1. statements to teacher not in response to questions
2. statements to other students not in response to questions
3. statements by students to expand on a topic
4. statements by students to start a new topic
5. imperatives
6. suggestions
7. exclamations

Discourse Management

1. requests for clarification: statements, questions, tag-questions
2. giving feedback to others: statements of agreement, apologies
3. social formulas: greetings and farewells

2. Questions and Answers

Statements and questions were classified into the following categories: general questions posed by the teacher to the entire class, specific questions posed by the teacher to individual students, general and specific questions posed by the students to the entire class or to particular class members; replies to general vs. specific questions from the teacher, replies to general vs. specific questions from fellow students, statements addressed to teacher or student(s) which were not in response to a question.

By far, the greatest number of entries were replies to questions (355), both to questions from the teacher as well as to questions from students. The replies to questions from the teacher outnumbered the replies to questions from fellow students by an almost 2-to-1 margin: there were not quite twice as many replies to the teacher's questions (229) as replies to other students' questions (126) - see Figure 1.

The second largest volume (176 questions were asked in the 14 sessions) of sentence type came in the form of students asking questions of other students (e.g., #1 below). There were fewer general questions posed by students to the entire group (54) and surprisingly fewer questions addressed to the instructor (26) - see Figure 2. Broken down by gender, it is interesting to note that men asked more general, open-ended questions to the whole group (40) than women did (14) and more questions of the teacher, men (19), women (7), as in #2 below. But in terms of specific questions to individual students, the sexes were more similar, with both women and men asking 88 questions - see Figure 3.

(1) *Stephen, warum fährst du nach San Antonio? Hast du Verwandte dort, oder kennst du Freunde dort?*

Stephen, why are you going to San Antonio? Do you have relatives there or do you know friends there?

(2) *Dr. Chun, was machen Sie dieses Wochenende? Sehen Sie einen Film? Ich habe gelesen, daß "Beauty and the Beast" sehr gut ist. Vielleicht wollen Ihre Kinder ihn sehen.*

Dr. Chun, what are you doing this weekend? Will you see a movie? I read that "Beauty and the Beast" is very good. Maybe your children will want to see it.

3. Statements and Imperatives

The third most common type of entry were statements addressed to other students (178), either to expand on a topic (#1 below), or to start a new topic (#2 below). This is significant because in traditional language classrooms, it is usually the teacher who is empowered to manage the discourse, but it seems that students are exercising their liberty to do so in CACD.

(1) *Aber A&M ist zu konservativ. Die Studenten tragen "Armystiefel."*	But [Texas] A&M [University] is too conservative. The students wear army boots.
(2) *Gestern habe ich einen neuen Job gefunden.*	Yesterday I found a new job.

A few imperatives (e.g., #3-5 below), often in the form of suggestions (e.g., #7 and #8 below), were produced. Similarly, some exclamations can be found, and certain students showed a tendency to use a fair amount of capitalization or exclamation points, presumably to indicate emphasis and enthusiasm, something which would / could be accomplished through the use of intonation in spoken language.

(3) *Besuchen Sie alle Iowa!*	You all [come] visit Iowa!
(4) *Chris ist krank. Hören Sie ihn nicht an!*	Chris is sick. Don't listen to him!
(6) *Vergeßt nicht, fleißig zu lernen!*	Don't forget to study hard!
(7) *Sehen wir* Beauty and the Beast *zusammen.*	Let's see *Beauty and the Beast* together.
(8) *Ich will nach Iowa fahren! Gehen wir zu Weihnachten dorthin!*	I want to go to Iowa. Let's do there for Christmas!

4. Discourse Management

In terms of discourse management during a discussion, turn-taking as done in spoken conversation is not a factor in CACD. However, other types of conversational strategies, such as capturing attention, taking the initiative, changing the subject or expanding on a topic can be examined. The data show that first and second semester students are also acquiring these types of competence (see Appendix 2). In a normal classroom, situations and contexts can be engineered to encourage oral discussion, but students are usually told what to talk about and what to ask the others in their group (e.g., "Ask group members 2 questions each about their families"). With CACD, a general topic for discussion is suggested at the beginning, but students have complete freedom as to whom to address, how to take the conversation further (e.g. with follow-up comments or questions), and when to change the subject if they wish. The data show that students do indeed take the initiative in CACD—see Figure 4: they directly address other students often with statements and questions (354 times in 14 sessions), e.g. #1 below and the teacher occasionally (only 46 times in 14 sessions). They do a marvelous job of expanding on a subject (482 statements and questions, e.g. #2 below, and they introduce new subjects as well (95 times in 14 sessions).

(1) *Jenny, wie finden Sie Ihren Job? Haben Sie jetzt genug Geld, so daß Sie nicht mehr arbeiten müssen?*	Jenny, how do you like your job? Do you have enough money so that you don't have to work any more?
(2) *Hat jemand nächstes Semester Mathematik 427?.*	Is anyone taking Math 427 next semester?
(3) *Mein Computer ist kaputt. Ich habe "Dink-Donk" gehört.*	My computer is broken. I heard "Ding-dong."

5. Requests for Clarification

Questions were rarely misunderstood, and when they were, requests for clarification were immediately forthcoming. Students used various syntactic constructions to do so: statements, e.g. #1 and #2 below; questions, e.g. #3-#7 below; and tag questions, e.g. #8 below. In Kramsch's terms, students were expressing, interpreting and negotiating meaning, granted on a very basic level, but they were nonetheless using appropriate rhetorical devices and discourse strategies.

(1) *Ich verstehe nicht.*	I don't understand.
(2) *Ich habe den Witz auch nicht verstanden.*	I didn't understand the joke either.
(3) *Was bedeutet ...?*	What does ... mean?
(4) *Was ist das?*	What is that?
(5) *Wie sagt man ...?*	How do you say ...?
(6) *Was meinst du, Jason? Ich bin nicht so alt.*	What do you mean, Jason? I'm not so old.
(7) *James, ist das eine Frage?*	James, is that a question?
(8) *In Deutschland trinken alle Leute Bier, ja?*	In Germany everyone drinks beer, right?

In addition, other tag-questions which stated and solicited opinions were used, e.g. #9 and #10 below, and a few rhetorical questions surfaced as well, e.g. #11 and #12 below:

(9) *Kim ist realistisch, ja?*	Kim is realistic, yes?
(10) *Das ist nicht sehr höflich, oder?*	That is not very polite, or? (That's not very polite, is it?)
(11) *Warum nicht?*	Why not?
(12) *Die Welt wird kleiner, ja?*	The world is getting smaller, isn't it?

6. Giving Feedback

Giving feedback to others is also a part of interactive competence, and students did it in various ways. Agreement with another was expressed, e.g. #1 below. Direct reference was made to what others had written, establishing coherence in the discourse, e.g. #2 below. An apology was offered once after someone had asked for clarification, e.g. #3 below. In the same sequence, after requesting clarification and receiving it, the student gave immediate feedback, see #4 below.

(1) *Ja, du hast recht.*	Yes, you're right.
(2) *Ich habe immer in den Städten gewohnt, wie Kim.*	I always lived in the cities, like Kim.
(3) *Es tut mir leid, daß ich es nicht erklärt habe.*	I'm sorry that I didn't explain it.
(4) *Ja, ich verstehe jetzt.*	Yes, I understand now.

7. Social Formulas

Many more leave-taking expressions and farewells (82) were produced than greetings (15), probably because the computer sessions were always done at the end of the class period. The greetings were usually very simple and often asked about or described how one was feeling, e.g. #1 and #2 below, and the farewells ranged from the standard 'Goodbye,' e.g. #3 below to explanations for why one had to leave, e.g. #4-#6 below:

(1) *Servus, meine Kollegen. Ich bin sehr müde.*	Hello, my colleagues. I'm very tired.
(2) *Hallo alle! Wie geht's?*	Hello all! How's it going?
(3) *Tschüß, bis morgen!*	Bye, till tomorrow!
(4) *Ich muß gehen, weil ich ein Interview habe. Schönes Wochenende.*	I have to go because I have an interview. Have a nice weekend.
(5) *Ich muß jetzt zur Bibliothek gehen, sonst bekomme ich eine Null für meine Hausaufgabe.*	I have to go to the library now or else I'll get a zero on my homework.
(6) *Ja, ich gehe auch bald. Ich bin immer spät. Mein Lehrer ist böse...*	Yes, I'm going soon, too. I'm always late. My teacher is angry...

IV. Summary and Conclusions

In summary, the data show that computer-assisted classroom discussion (CACD) provides excellent opportunities for foreign language learners to develop the discourse skills and interactive competence advocated by the *ACTFL Proficiency Guidelines* and amended by Kramsch (1986). And as Raimes (1992) suggests for improving writing, learners must not only be able to read and follow the threads of ongoing, multi-participant discussions, but they must initiate and communicate real messages as well as expand on topics begun by others. A decided advantage of CACD is that learners are under neither time pressure to respond nor the psychological pressure of making a mistake or looking foolish. In addition, the length and breadth of their entries are not restricted, and their individual styles are allowed to flourish.

One of the most striking features of the quantitative and qualitative data from first- and second-semester German students is that the students interact directly with each other, as opposed to interacting mainly with the teacher. In typical, traditional classroom discourse, the bulk of student utterances are answers to questions from the teacher. In my data from the 14 sessions of CACD, there were 355 students' replies to questions and 256 student-initiated questions asked of others. If the number of statements addressed to others (198) is added to the number of questions asked (256), then the total (454) is greater than the number of replies to questions and demonstrates that learners are definitely taking the initiative, constructing and expanding on topics and taking a more active role in discourse management than is typically found in normal classroom discussion. In addition, learners exhibit the ability to give feedback to other, as well as sociolinguistic competence in greeting and leave taking, requesting confirmation or clarification, and apologizing.

The types of sentences being written by students on the computer require not only comprehension of the preceding discourse but also coherent thought and use of cohesive linguistic references and expressions. These skills, which are important components of writing proficiency, are enhanced by CACD. In addition, since these types of sentences strongly resemble what would be said in a spoken conversation, the hope is that the written competence gained from CACD can gradually be transferred to the students' speaking competence as well. The computer is thus proving itself to be an effective medium for facilitating the acquisition of interactive competence in writing and speaking. Furthermore, it is an excellent research tool for collecting data and documenting student thought processes and progress in learning a second language.

Notes

[1]Underwood (1987, pp. 413-414) was one of the first to use electronic mail with a Spanish conversation course and found that it "proved to be a vehicle for communicative practice on a large scale." Since then, numerous other uses have been reported, cf., for example, Barson, Frommer, & Schwartz, 1993; Brammerts, 1996; Kern, 1996; Warschauer, 1995a.

[2]Cf. Beauvois, 1992; Bump, 1990; Chávez, 1997; Cononelos & Oliva, 1992; Kelm, 1992, 1996; Kern, 1995; Lunde, 1990; Ortega, 1997; Slatin, 1991; Warschauer 1996a, 1997.

[3]CLP is a term suggested by Bachman & Savignon (1986, p. 382) to incorporate the principles of both the communicative competence and proficiency movements.

[4]Swaffar (1992) personal communication.

[5]Cf. Canale &Swain (1980) and Omaggio (1986) for descriptions of the four major components of *communicative competence*. Omaggio (1986:7-8) summarizes these different types of competence: "*Grammatical competence* refers to the degree to which the language user has mastered the linguistic code... *Sociolinguistic competence* addresses the extent to which grammatical forms can be used or understood appropriately in various contexts to convey specific communicative functions, such as persuading, describing, narrating, and giving commands... *Discourse competence...* involves the ability to combine ideas to achieve cohesion in form and coherence in thought... *Strategic competence...* involves the use of verbal and nonverbal communication strategies to compensate for gaps in the language user's knowledge of the code."

Cf. Magnan (1988) for a discussion of grammar and the ACTFL Proficiency Interview (OPI) and also Koike (1989, p. 279) on L2 learners' *pragmatic competence* in interlanguage. Koike defines pragmatic competence as "the speaker's knowledge and use of rules of appropriateness and politeness which dictate the way the speaker will understand and formulate speech acts."

[6]Cf. Omaggio (1986, pp. 12-13), who describes three integrated criteria which are said to underlie proficiency descriptions: "the linguistic *functions* an individual is typically able to express, the *contexts* or *content areas* (topics) that can be discussed, and the degree of *accuracy* with which the message can be communicated."

[7]We have chosen the intermediate level because it appears that above average students can reach that level after one year of college instruction.

[8]Cf. Barker & Kemp, 1990; Ferrera, Brunner, & Whittemore, 1991; Greenia, 1992; Scott, 1990; Sullivan & Pratt, 1996.

[9]Cf. Gerrard, 1987; Batson, 1988, 1989; Faigley, 1990.

[10]Cf. Beauvois, 1992. Since that time many studies have been reported on. Kern (1995), for one, investigated the structuring classroom interaction with networked computers and found interesting effects on quantity and characteristics of language production. Cf. Ortega, 1997; Warschauer, 1996a.

[11]Cf. Richards, Platt, & Weber. *Longman Dictionary of Applied Linguistics* (1985, pp. 265-6) for Categories of **Speech Acts** ["a speech act is an utterance as a *functional* unit in communication"]:

1) **directives**: begging, commanding, requesting
2) **commissives**: promising, guaranteeing, threatening
3) **expressives**: apologising, welcoming, sympathising, thanking, congratulating, complaining, complimenting
4) **declarations**: christening, marrying, resigning
5) **representatives**: asserting, hypothesising, describing

[12]Cf. Omaggio (1986, pp. 16-18), who also lists further types of competence, occasionally evidenced in part by some of our first-year students: 1) At the Advanced (2/2+) level: "They can participate fully in casual conversations, expressing facts, giving instructions, describing places, people, and things, reporting on events, and providing narration about past, present, and future activities . . . . Their discourse competence is also improved as they continue to use longer and more complex sentence structure to express their meaning." At the Superior level, "They can handle unknown topics and situations, give supported opinions, hypothesize, provide complicated explanations, describe in detail with a great deal of precision . . . ."

[13]One of the students, a graduate student who teaches French, remarked enthusiastically after the first session "This is real communication!"

[14]An attempted "translation" of an expression in English resulted in a humorous entry: *John, du weißt , was sie sagen, 'Quatsch in, Quatsch aus,* "John, you know what they say, 'Garbage in, garbage out."

References

Bachman, L. F., & Savignon, S. J. (1986). The evaluation of communicative language proficiency: A critique of the ACTFL Oral Interview. *Modern Language Journal, 70,* 380-90.

Barker, T. T., & Kemp, F. O. (1990). Network theory: A postmodern pedagogy for the writing classroom. In C. Handa (Ed.), *Computers and community: Teaching composition in the twenty-first century* (pp. 1-27). Portsmouth: Boynton/Cook.

Barnett, M. A. (1989). Writing as a process. *The French Review, 63*(1), 31-44.

Barson, J., Frommer, J., & Schwartz, M. (1993). Foreign language learning using e-mail in a task-oriented perspective: Inter-university experiments in communication and collaboration. *Journal of Science Education and Technology, 2*(4), 565-584.

Batson, T. W. (1988). The ENFI project: A networked classroom approach to writing instruction. *Academic Computing* February, 32-33, 55-56.

Batson, T. W. (Ed.). (1989). Proposal abstracts from the 5th Computers and Writing Conference, University of Minnesota, Minneapolis, May 12-14, 1989. Washington, D.C.: Gallaudet University.

Beauvois, M. H. (1992). Computer-assisted classroom discussion in the foreign language classroom: Conversation in slow motion. *Foreign Language Annals, 25*(5), 455-464.

Brammerts, H. (1996). Language learning in tandem using the Internet. In M. Warschauer (Ed.), *Telecollaboration in Foreign Language Learning* (pp. 121-130). Honolulu: Second Language Teaching & Curriculum Center, University of Hawai'i.

Bump, J. (1990). Radical changes in class discussion using networked computers. *Computers and the Humanities, 24,* 49-65.

Byrnes, H. (1987). Proficiency as a framework for research in second language acquisition. *Modern Language Journal, 71,* 44-49.

Canale, M., & Swain, M. (1980). Theoretical bases of communicative approaches to second language teaching and testing. *Applied Linguistics, 1,* 1-47.

Chávez, C. L. (1997). Students take flight with Daedalus: Learning Spanish in a networked classroom. *Foreign Language Annals, 30*(1), 27-37.

Cononelos, T., & Oliva, M. (1992). Using the networks in advanced foreign language classes. *Computers and Composition Digest* [on-line] , University of Utah.

Faigley, L. (1990). Subverting the electronic workbook: Teaching writing using networked computers. *The Writing Teacher as Researcher: Essays in the Theory of Class-Based Writing.* Upper-Montclair, NJ: Heinemann-Boynton.

Ferrara, K., Brunner, H., & Whittemore, G. (1991). Interactive written discourse as an emergent register. *Written Communication, 8* (1), 9-33.

Gerrard, L. (Ed.). (1987). *Writing at Century's End: Essays on Computer-Assisted Composition.* New York: Random House.

Greenia, G. D. (1992). Computers and teaching composition in a foreign language. *Foreign Language Annals, 25*(1), 33-45.

Herring, S. (Ed.). (1996). *Computer-mediated communication: Linguistic, social, and cross-cultural perspectives.* Amsterdam: John Benjamins.

Kaiser, M. (1997). Digital technologies and foreign language pedagogy: New tools and new paradigms? Berkeley Language Center Symposium, Berkeley.

Kelm, O. R. (1992). The use of synchronous computer networks in second language instruction: A preliminary report. *Foreign Language Annals, 25*(5), 441-454.

Kelm, O. R. (1996). The application of computer networking in foreign language education: Focusing on principles of second language acquisition. In M. Warschauer (Ed.), *Telecollaboration in Foreign Language Learning* (pp. 19-28). Honolulu: Second Language Teaching & Curriculum Center, University of Hawai'i.

Kern, R. G. (1995). Restructuring classroom interaction with networked computers: Effects on quantity and characteristics of language production. *The Modern Language Journal, 79*(4), 457-476.

Kern, R. G. (1996). Computer-mediated communication: Using e-mail exchanges to explore personal histories in two cultures. In M. Warschauer (Ed.), *Telecollaboration in Foreign Language Learning* (pp. 105-119). Honolulu: Second Language Teaching & Curriculum Center, University of Hawaii.

Koike, D. A. (1989). Pragmatic competence and adult L2 acquisition: Speech acts in interlanguage. *Modern Language Journal, 73*(3), 279-289.

Kramsch, C. J. (1983). Interaction in the classroom: Learning to negotiate roles and meanings. *Die Unterrichtspraxis, 16*(2), 175-190.

Kramsch, C. J. (1986). From language proficiency to interactional competence. *Modern Language Journal, 70*, 366-372.

Kramsch, C. J. (Ed.). (1995). *Context and culture in language teaching.* Oxford: Oxford University Press.

Lunde, K. (1990). Using electronic mail as a medium for foreign language study and instruction. *CALICO Journal, 7*(3), 68-78.

Magnan, S. S. (1988). Grammar and the ACTFL oral proficiency interview: Discussion and data. *Modern Language Journal, 72*(3), 266-276.

Markley, P. (1992). *A look at computer networking designed for composition, its goals in the classroom, and its impact on gender and cultural roles.* Unpublished manuscript.

Omaggio, A. C. (1986). *Teaching language in context.* Boston: Heinle & Heinle.

Ortega, L. (1997). Processes and outcomes in networked classroom interaction: Defining the research agenda for L2 computer-assisted classroom discussion. *Language Learning and Technology 1* (1), 82-93.

Raimes, A. (1992). *Exploring through writing: A process approach to ESL composition.* New York: St. Martin's Press.

Richards, J., Platt, J., & Weber, H. (1985). *Longman dictionary of applied linguistics.* Harlow: Longman.

Scott, V. (1990). Task-oriented creative writing with Systeme-D. *CALICO Journal* 7(3), 58-67.

Slatin, J. (1991). *Forum sessions: Real-time, on-line communication and the formation of a discourse community: The computer as instructional medium in an English composition classroom.* Unpublished manuscript.

Sullivan, N., & Pratt, E. (1996). A comparative study of two ESL writing environments: A computer-assisted classroom and a traditional oral classroom. *System, 19*, 491-501.

Underwood, J. (1987). Correo: Electronic mail as communicative practice. *Hispania, 70*, 413-414.

Warschauer, M. (1995a). *E-mail for English teaching*. Alexandria, VA: TESOL.

Warschauer, M. (Ed.) (1995b). *Virtual connections.* Honolulu: Second Language Teaching and Curriculum Center, University of Hawaii.

Warschauer, M. (1996a). Comparing face to face and electronic discussion in the second language classroom. *CALICO Journal, 13*(2&3), 7-26.

Warschauer, M. (Ed.). (1996b). *Telecollaboration in foreign language learning*. Honolulu: Second Language Teaching & Curriculum Center, University of Hawai'i.

Warschauer, M. (1997). Computer-mediated collaborative learning: Theory and practice. *Modern Language Journal, 81*(4), 470-481.

FIGURE 1. GREATEST NUMBER OF ENTRIES

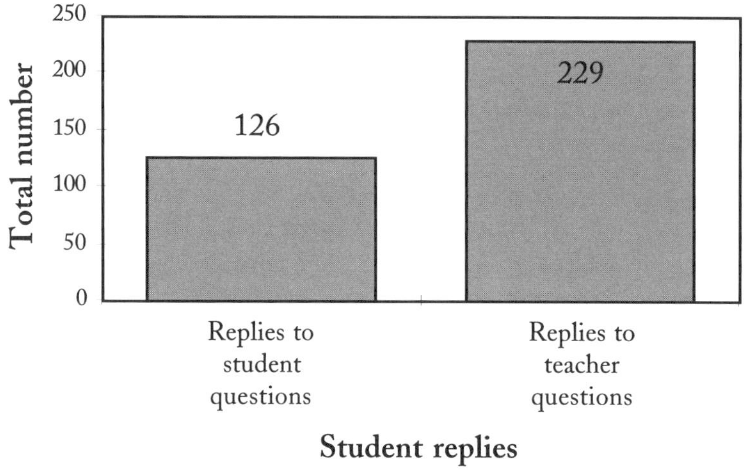

FIGURE 2. SECOND LARGEST NUMBER OF ENTRIES

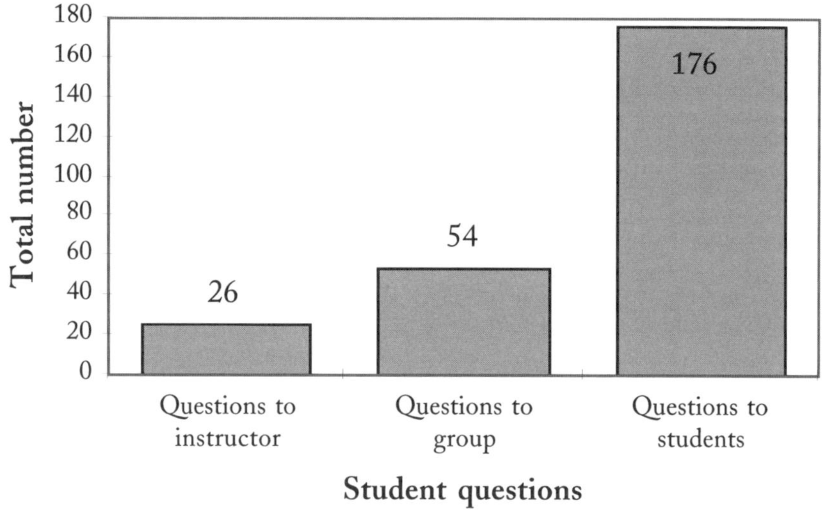

FIGURE 3. STUDENT ENTRIES BY GENDER

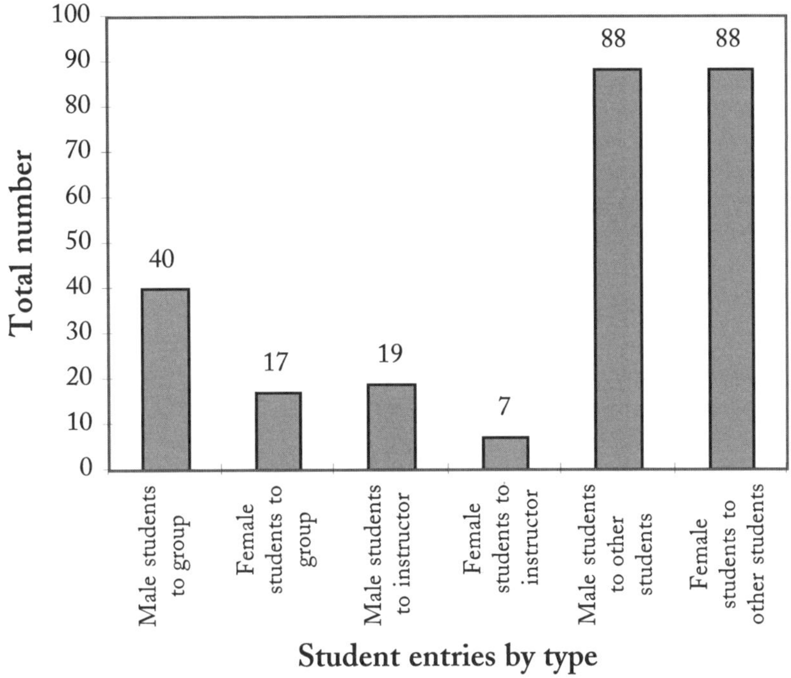

FIGURE 4. DISCOURSE MANAGEMENT

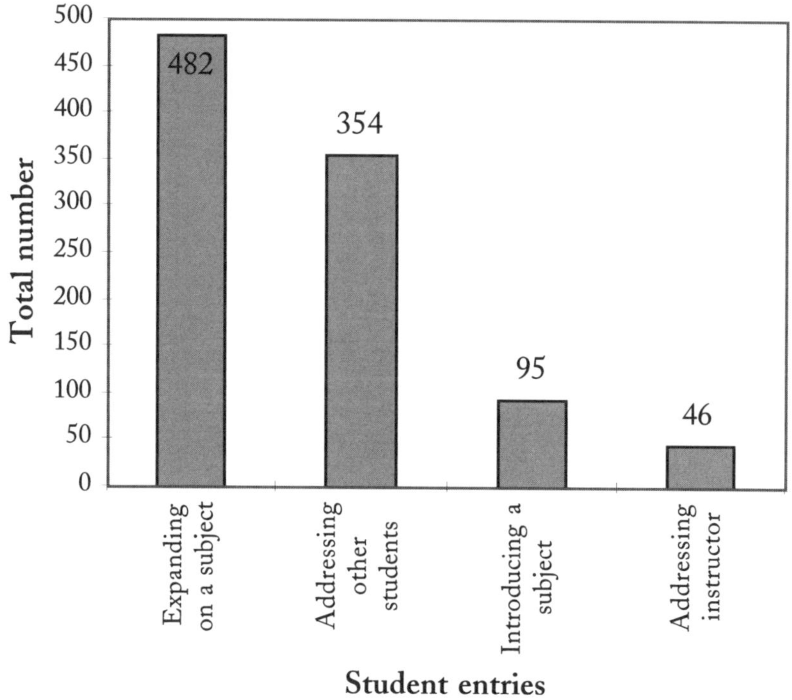

Appendix 1

Student	Sex	10/30/91	11/8/91	11/15/91	11/22/91	12/4/92	Average fall	Average spring	Fall and spring
CB	M	26	18		20	7	17.8		17.8
GH	F	5	6	3			4.7		4.7
DK	M	12	12	7	12	8	10.2	7.9	9.0
SL	M	10	7		8	6	7.8		7.8
JM	M	4	7	5	3	12	6.2	8.0	7.1
HM	F	18	14	9	14		13.8		13.8
JM	F		7		7	9	7.7		7.7
JP	M	7		6		9	7.3	7.0	7.2
AJP	M	8	9	4	9	11	8.2	7.3	7.8
NK	F	8	7	5		6	6.5	4.0	5.3
MS	F	1		2	2	4	2.3	3.3	2.8
TS	F	7	7	3	10	10	7.4		7.4
LS	F	4	6	4	7	8	5.8	9.6	7.7
KT	F	6	7	5	9	7	6.8	4.8	5.8
MU	M							14.1	14.1
Average		**8.9**	**8.9**	**4.8**	**9.2**	**8.1**	**8.0**	**7.3**	**8.4**

	1/31/92	2/4/92	2/14/92	2/26/92	3/7/92	3/31/92	4/10/92	4/24/92	5/1/92
DK	6	8	6	9	7	12	4	12	7
JM	7	8		5	8	12	7		9
JP	7	6	6	4	7	9		9	8
AJP	4	6	8	5	5	13	9	10	6
NR	4	4	5	3		2	6		
MS	2	2	2	2	1	8	4	6	3
LS	8	5	11	9	9	14	6	16	8
KT	1	5	4		3	7	5	6	7
MU	13	11	8	12	15	18	15	21	14

Appendix 2

Utterance Type	Totals (M=26, F=33) 1st Semester	Totals (M=42, F=32) 2nd Semester	Grand Totals
greeting	5	10	15
farewell	38	44	82
reply to general question from teacher	81	92	173
reply to specific question from teacher	25	31	56
reply to general question from student	8	9	17
reply to specific question from student	73	36	109
statement (addressed to student)	98	80	178
statement (addressed to teacher)	5	15	20
general yes-no question	7	8	15
general wh-question	20	19	39
specific yes-no question (addressed to student)	57	30	87
specific wh-question (addressed to student)	67	22	89
specific yes-no question (teacher addressee)	3	7	10
specific wh-question (teacher addressee)	4	12	16
general imperative/suggestion	9	7	16
specific imperative/suggestion	8	10	18
exclamation	18	28	46
use of !	69	21	90
simple statement	161	399	560
compound/complex sentence	48	297	345
introduction of new topic/ [with question]	28	15	43
change of topic [with statement]	20	32	52
expanding on topic (with question)	53	23	76
expanding on topic (with statement)	37	369	406
request for clarification (with question)	22	23	45
request for confirmation (with statement)	2	5	7

Empowering Students: The Diverse Roles of Asians and Women in the ESL Computer Classroom

Phillip Markley

Introduction

Two predominant issues have emerged in recent work on the learner-centered ESL classroom. The first issue is part of the ongoing research in L1 and L2 studies about the positive effects of learner-centered instruction (Doughtery, & Pica, 1986; Gaies,1983; Long, Adams, McLean, & Castaños, 1976; Peterson, Wilkinson, & Hallinan, 1983; Pica, & Doughtery, 1985; Rulon, & McCreary, 1986). Most of this research, however, usually juxtaposes the learner-centered classroom with its peer group discussions and teacher-centered or fronted classrooms. That is, it looks at classroom interactions with a specific agenda in mind, such as making recommendations about breaking the cycle of teacher talk in order to promote learner inquiry.

The second issue for research is the learner-centered classroom itself, specifically, the dynamics and outcomes of its distinctive pedagogy. This focus has yielded two particularly interesting bodies of research, suggesting that the learner-centered classroom may not work in the same way across all student populations. More specifically, it seems that (1) Asians (in my sample, Chinese, Japanese, and Koreans) find it difficult to participate in learner-centered classes, and that (2) gender may be a factor in students' participation (especially among Asian females, but not confined to females in this ethnic group).

For example, Sato's (1981) research points out that in international ESL classrooms where Asians outnumbered non-Asians, Asians took significantly fewer turns in classroom interactions. This tendency indicates that many students from different cultural backgrounds may be less direct about confronting the teacher and often fall into the practice of only listening to the teacher and never questioning. In addition, recent research has explored the correlations between gendered behavior and cultural background (Heath, 1992; Shackle, 1987; Smith, 1987). In one of the most significant of these studies, Heath specifically outlines traditional roles of Asian women which may reflect some of their timid behavior in the school classroom. Clearly, either of these limitations on classroom behaviors will impact on the efficacy and success of the learner-centered classroom.

More recently, assertions have been made about the roles that computer classrooms may play, in light of these two major issues about possible ethnic and gender restrictions in classroom behaviors. The first of these assertions is that Computer-Assisted Classroom Discussion (CACD) is a possible positive alternative to teacher-centered classrooms because CACD classrooms place more power to control classroom interactions in the hands of the students. This style of learner-centered classroom breaks the cycle of teacher-centered classrooms found in many L1 (cf. Bellack, Kliebard, Hyman, & Smith., 1966; Dunkin, & Biddle, 1974) as well as L2 classrooms (cf. Chun, 1994; Kern, 1995; Legaretta, 1977; Ramirez, Yuen, Ramey, & Merino, 1986). The second assertion based on emerging research results is that the CACD can reduce some of the negative effects of classroom interactions from cultural background and/or gender (Ma, 1996; Sato, 1981; Shackle, 1987).

This chapter offers data to support both of these recent assertions. A set of parallel English composition classes in networked computer classrooms at the University of Texas at Austin suggests that, with careful instructional management, the CACD environment, defined here as a networking class, can offer effective learner-centered experiences. Networking seems to address at least some of the asymmetries associated with learned ethnic and gendered behavior patterns that persist in more conventional (i.e., non-CACD), albeit learner-centered, classrooms.

I. Context of the Experiment

The data analyzed in this paper are samplings taken from two different networking transcripts written during the 1991 / 92 academic year at the University of Texas at Austin. The student subjects for this study were in two English composition courses designed for first-year international students with TOEFL scores between 550 and 600. Both courses had the same teacher, met at the same hour of the day (in different semesters), and had the same number of class hours in a semester. The classroom sessions were 50 minutes in length and took place in the English Department Computer Laboratory, which consists of 22 computers networked in a LAN (local area network), and which are arranged in a U-shaped formation around the periphery of a large room with no windows (see Chapter 1, Slatin's discussion of the computer laboratory facilities).

Most of the students in these courses were freshmen or sophomores who were required to take the course; however, a few were graduate students wanting to improve their composition skills. The ages of the subjects thus ranged from around eighteen to forty. Many of the students were Asians, particularly native speakers of Chinese (see Appendices 1 and 2 for class breakdowns). Their nationality and cultural background was ascertainable through information supplied to me by the University of Texas at Austin. In addition, as a supplement to this data, I interviewed students in the study informally about their language and ethnicity. The students confirmed, too, that their main goal for the class (whether required or optional) was to improve their English composition skills.

The classes were designed to aid students in achieving these goals by consciously adopting a learner-centered pedagogy. As is familiar, learner-centered approaches structure classroom settings where students talk to one another rather than exclusively to the teacher. As noted, however, such patterns are relatively foreign to many ESL students. Chaudron (1988), for example, states that research on classes with ethnic minorities illustrates differential cultural expectations for the manner of participation in school classrooms (e.g., Brophy, & Good, 1974; Cazden, John, & Hymes, 1972; Laosa, 1979; Philips, 1972; cf. also Sullivan, this volume; Trueba, Guthrie, & Hu-pei,1981). Nonetheless, a learner-centered approach to the problem of improving English composition still seemed appropriate for these courses, given the wide range of students' ages and abilities represented. To accommodate the diverse audience, the syllabus included many activity types. Regardless of the task at hand, however, the teacher was clearly defined as a facilitator for student writing rather than as an authority about "proper" writing.

Although many different classroom activities might be defined as "learner-centered," current research in L1 and L2 stresses the importance of dialogue as a bridge to writing for display (under rubrics like "writing for learning"; see, for example, Raimes, 1991). One consistently-employed activity available within the Daedalus software used by this class was computer conferencing as an alternative to whole class networking (for detailed explanation, see Chapter l). By clicking on "Join a Conference" rather than "InterChange" under the activity menu, student-generated question / answer sessions could be structured as small-group dialogs. Small conferences create somewhat more synchronous exchanges than those possible when the whole class networks together. Individual students who can collaborate or respond in this fashion have more control over the focus for writing than they do in asynchronous networking where many participants write at the same time. When these conference activities were carried out in the networking classroom, two subgroups who are traditionally less successful in participating in such activities—women and Asians—were particularly encouraged to participate and expand their role in classroom communication.

II. Research Design

As already noted, L1 and L2 studies have indicated the general positive effects of learner-centered instruction (Doughtery, & Pica, 1986; Gaies, 1983; Long, Adams, McLean, & Castaños, 1976; Peterson, Wilkinson, & Hallinan, 1983; Pica, & Doughtery, 1985; Rulon, & McCreary, 1986). Research by Heath and Sato, however, indicates that not all cultural groups respond equally to the same classroom conditions. The class situation just described allowed a more differentiated approach to the research question about the possible impacts that a learner-centered classroom in a CACD environment may have on female and Asian students in these classrooms.

By comparing two InterChange session transcripts from the 1991/92 academic year, it is possible to sort out, quantitative and qualitative correspondences between responses, gender, and cultural background.[1] Both InterChange transcripts analyzed represent one sample class out of a full semester, one from the fall semester and a second from the spring. These two transcripts were analyzed separately on the basis of number of entries and gender of individuals making those entries. Those averages, in turn, were scrutinized for individual differences. Most students in both classes, over seventy percent in the fall class, ninety percent in the spring class, had been born and educated in Asian countries (see Appendix 2). Consequently, both the fall and spring classes offered a large enough subject group to allow some preliminary conclusions about gender-dispersed behaviors: there was a large enough mix of male and female subjects from Asian backgrounds to explore how the well-documented culturally-imposed gendered behaviors affect classroom behaviors.

This class composition enabled a qualitative analysis of specific student groups' behaviors within a given pedagogical framework. Moreover, since session transcripts are complete and offered in real-time order, it is possible to evolve a quantitative measure of classroom behavior, based on the number of sentences or lines written by each student. Analyzing the session transcripts allows a reasonably accurate account of student participation in this networked, learner-centered environment, as well as facilitating observations about the impact of the computer and of teacher input.

InterChange 1 was conducted during the Fall of 1991, in a class of over 90% Asians from Pacific Rim nations. A text by Malcom X was selected to help develop among foreign students who knew little or nothing about African-American culture a sense of the values and problems faced by African-Americans. The students read a short article by Malcolm X, called "Hair," where he explained "conking," the process of straightening thick curly hair. The classroom dialogue was designed to help these students create schema for "conking." As its starting point, the computer class addressed the concept of beauty and questioned how different individuals felt about socially-created norms for beauty (e.g., tatoos, artificially straight or curly hair, breast implants).

The discussion that followed the reading was structured largely as a question-and-answer session. At first glance, gender and cultural background appear to play a minimal role in class participation in InterChange 1. Figure 1 based on InterChange 1 (see below) showed that females and males were very similar in classroom participation. However, as the discussion below indicates, if Figure 1 is further broken down (see Figures 2 and 3 below), some differences in female and male participation in the class emerge.

IIIa. Quantitative Results

A quantitative break-down of InterChange for the fall class suggests how gender roles affect classroom dynamics.. Each line of output used as a statistical unit represents 7 to 9 typed words, but does not always equal a complete sentence. The mean average number lines written by both male and female students were virtually equivalent.

14 Males averaged 19.8 = 20 lines	7 Females averaged 18.5 = 19 lines

FIGURE 1. FALL CLASS: AVERAGE NUMBER OF LINES WRITTEN FOR A SINGLE INTERCHANGE

In terms of raw averages, then, there appears to be little inequality in participation between the male and female students in this particular InterChange. However, after these averages are broken down into performance subgroupings by gender, instead of a group average for each gender, a different picture of classroom behavior emerges.

When the sample was grouped according to those who wrote nineteen or more lines, those who wrote between eleven and eighteen lines, and those who wrote ten or fewer lines, a different picture emerges.

Females who have written 19 lines or more	1	14%
Females who have written 11-18 lines	3	43%
Females who have written 10 or fewer lines	3	43%

FIGURE 2. TOTAL NUMBER OF FEMALES IN THE FALL 1991 CLASS = 7

This tri-part breakdown gives some insight into possible gender-based differences in performance in an environment largely conditioned by the students' shared cultural background. Fully 86% of the female students are below the class average of nineteen lines per student written per period although three of these were just below the average number of lines written. Thus, whereas overall averages indicate that female participation seems to be equal to male participation; more individualized assessment suggests that female participation in the class is effectively lower, and varies greatly by individual, running generally below the class average—forming, in essence, the bottom half of the class in quantity of production.

The picture becomes bleaker when one looks at the single female student who wrote above the class average of 19 lines. This individual actually wrote a phenomenal 47 lines during this InterChange. She was a Korean student who was one of the few women in a scientific field of study that in Korea is predominantly male, and so she may well have more opportunities to express her opinions even with her male colleagues. In a follow-up interview, she identified her behavior was unusual by Korean standards, and that many of her female friends criticized her for being outspoken. If her statistics were removed from the female total on these grounds, even the global average for female participation in this class would be significantly less than that of male participants.

This Korean student and other women interviewed also tended to stress that each woman's level of education probably played a key role in her ability to compete or collaborate with fellow male students. Whether true or not, such self-reporting suggests that these women knew, at least in general terms, which of their cultural expectations they were or were not living up to. This inference, in turn, suggests that teachers in such mixed-gender and inter-ethnic classes may need to adapt different teaching strategies more consciously, depending on the previously learned gender and educational roles of their students. They may need to encourage participants to give themselves permission to act in a manner that they view as appropriate only among American students.

A turn to the equivalent statistics for the male students in this same InterChange only confirms the gender differentiations in quantity of language production.

Males who have written 19 lines or more	6	42%
Males who have written 11-18 lines	5	36%
Males who have written 10 or fewer lines	3	18%

Figure 3. Total Number of Males in the Fall 1991 Class = 14

According to Figure 3, 54% of the male students were below the average of nineteen lines written, compared to 86% of the female students. This difference in percentages confirms that the average male is participating more actively than the average female.

It should be emphasized that these results were achieved in spite of the teacher's conscious attempt at creating a student-centered environment that would be gender neutral. Although himself a man, because the teacher was also interacting on the computer network, personal factors such as size, voice pitch or volume, or seating order, factors that encourage equal participation among other groups, seemed to have little effect here.

The second InterChange transcript analyzed is from the subsequent spring semester. This class session met one semester later in a commensurate point in the syllabus. This second class was also predominantly composed of Chinese speakers (71% Asians from Pacific Rim nations). The other 29% were students from Latin America, Europe, and the Middle East (see Appendix 2). The discussion was also conducted on the basis of the students' reading of Malcolm X's "Hair," but the detail of the focus had changed somewhat. While the first class read "Hair" to understand African-American notions of beauty, the second class had read and discussed it earlier in the semester, and now compared it to " A Slow Walk of Trees" by Toni Morrison. Rather than discussing concepts of beauty, as had been true for the fall classes' transcript, the task for the spring class was to compare the articles. Perhaps as a direct result of this different task structure (which will be addressed in a later section on teacher performance), this second class had very different participation averages for male and female students, as seen in Figure 4 (and isolated in Figures 5 and 6 for purposes of further comparison with the transcript from the fall class).

13 Males averaged 17.9 = 18 lines	6 Females averaged 28.6 = 29 lines

FIGURE 4. SPRING CLASS: AVERAGE NUMBER OF LINES WRITTEN FOR A SINGLE INTERCHANGE

Starting from the average number of lines written, the transcript for the spring class InterChange reveals averages that contrast sharply with those of the fall class. The average number of lines for the fall InterChange was 20 for the males and nineteen for the females. The spring InterChange, however, shows an increase of 65% in total female participation in the network, with a concurrent 10% decrease in male participation. A breakdown in Figure 5 by performance groups reveals even more startling contrasts.

Females who have written 19 lines or more	5	83%
Females who have written 11-18 lines	1	17%
Females who have written 10 or fewer lines	0	0%

FIGURE 5. TOTAL NUMBER OF FEMALES IN SPRING 1991 CLASS = 6

The total number of females writing 19 lines or more were five. These five females represent a 69% increase in quantitative participation by females in the 19 lines or more category, compared to averages from the fall class. In the remaining two categories, there was one woman who had written 11-18 lines (a decrease of 26%), and no women in the 10 lines or less category (a decrease of 43%). In other words, in this InterChange session, 83% of the females fell into the highest category of lines written, thus decreasing both the 11-18 and 10 or fewer lines-written categories.

Potentially even more significant for this case is that the one student who remained in the "11-18 lines written" category was a Chinese woman from Argentina. In her follow-up interview, she stated that her upbringing was very traditionally Chinese. Thus this student would agree that her lack of participation correlates with her cultural background, which agrees with earlier observations (Heath, 1992; Sato,1981): she, like a number of Asians (and particularly female Asians, as we see here), expressed timidity about participating in class.

Although female participation patterns changed drastically in the two classes, as figure 5 reveals, male participation patterns conform more closely to those of men in the preceding semester.

Males who have written 19 lines or more	6	46%
Males who have written 11-18 lines	5	38%
Males who have written 10 or fewer lines	2	15%

FIGURE 6. TOTAL NUMBER OF MALES IN THE SPRING 1992 CLASS = 13

Male participation in both InterChange sessions thus remained very similar. The male participation category "19 lines or more" fell 4%, while "11-18 lines written" increased 2% and "10 lines or fewer" category increased 3%. The two males who fell into the category of lowest participation were native speakers of Chinese (again corresponding with results from Heath, 1992 and Sato, 1981); with one exception, the same was true for the middle category of "11-18 lines." Since male participation in both classes remained relatively stable, quite possibly the two InterChange tasks were perceived in approximately the same way by males in both classes.

The difference in female participation, however, prompts looking at this assumption in more detail. The easiest explanation of the difference in female participation is that in the second class, the women were less dominantly of Asian cultural heritage than the males (only 50% Asian), and so were less constrained by stereotypes of non-participation than their largely Asian male counterparts (92% Asian and Chinese speakers).

In both cases, however, the CACD format did not seem to have the expected effect of balancing gender contributions in the classroom (see Sullivan, this volume): in a relatively unmixed group of students (those who share more cultural heritage than not, such as heavy concentrations of Asian students), the students may not respond to "student-centeredness" in the same way as more conventional US classes (which are often extremely culture-mixed and / or have mixed in their educational habits, as were the females in the spring 1992 class).

IIIb. Pedagogical Framework for the Quantitative Results

While the quantitative results of this comparison between a homogeneous and a culturally heterogeneous class may not be absolutely suggestive, a qualitative analysis of the pedagogical framework of the InterChange sessions reveals how the acknowledged advantages of a computer-adapted class may nonetheless be incorporated into situations that more actively involve cultural and gender-specific variables.

The results reported here suggest that structuring an InterChange class in student-responsive ways may be essential in order to capitalize on the advantages inherent in the CACD environment and to enhance participation, across cultural and gendered lines. Teacher interventions can be used to create specific classroom dynamics. For example, gender seems to play a role in predicting the lack of participation by women and particularly by some Asian women, as discussed here. To overcome this possible disparity in class participation on the basis of gender, the teacher may have to create question(s) specifically for women, "requiring" their participation. The effect of such targeted questioning is not only to "help students with their writing," but also to authorize their stepping beyond their tacit cultural norms, or to reset those norms for their particular personae and personal needs in the new language and culture. In this instance, the Asian women participating on InterChange need not "behave" verbally the way women do in the United States, but they need to realize that Asian politeness is often read as extreme reticence, or even diffidence, by many North American speakers. To become more communicative in this environment, then, an individual Asian student (male or female) might benefit by realizing that participation in a discussion in the United States is not only acceptable, but desirable. To foster such participation in a networked classroom, four styles of teacher management are suggested here.

1) Asking reticent participants as a group for their reactions to a given topic. In addressing culture-bound inhibitions, the teacher does not need to preach to or reprogram students, but merely overtly signal what is understood covertly in the target culture. For example, Malcolm X discussed "conking" as the physical mutilation of the body to arrive at a societal standard. To remind students that this issue tacitly rests on gender issues as well as aesthetic ones, and that both genders need to participate in this discussion, the teacher of the English composition class reported on here introduced a new computer assignment for the female students the next time the text was taught:

```
What do the women in the class think about
physical mutilation of the body in order to
obtain a 'beautiful' body?  Do you think
that women have more pressure to conform to
societal standards than men?  Explain.
```

By consciously engaging the "women in the class" instead of just the "class" (stressing overtly that the women were part of the class), this assignment prompted female students to increase the quantity of their written participation. Instead of the women writing an average number of nineteen lines per student (an overall student average in multiple InterChange classes), the female students in this session increased their input to twenty-two lines per woman.

2) Including readings that invite comparison. In the spring class, assignments were modified to raise what was culturally tacit in writing assignments to the level of cultural explicitness. Adding Toni Morrison's article "A Slow Walk of Trees" to the syllabus already containing Malcolm X's "Hair" encouraged students to consider the questions of gender and racism more actively, when they compared how each author analyzed and related social causes and effects. "Hair" is a man's perspective on acculturated standards of beauty—an issue usually considered "more naturally relevant" to women. In addition, "A Slow Walk of Trees" is explicitly about racism and also contains strong women characters that conceivably appealed to a female audience looking across cultural boundaries. This shift to an explicit management of gender participation by the teacher/facilitator may have contributed to the rise of 65% in female participation between the two sessions analyzed here (Figure 4).

3) Acknowledging indirect as well as directed forms of address. That this facilitation technique was so dramatically successful may have also been a direct result of the CACD as much as explicit teacher intervention. The option in the InterChange environment to participate without a direct exchange with another student or the teacher was of particular advantage in the cross-cultural context explored here, and may also have encouraged more interaction on all levels. Indeed, review of both transcripts suggests that students in the classes described here seemed to be most comfortable in a general mode, addressing no specific person.

By using the general "Student - Class" address for most messages participants could avoid naming names and circumvent direct confrontations, while still actually engaging in a discussion. When individuals address the class as a whole in this way, they share their unique insights with their classmates. If a teacher wishes to follow cooperative learning techniques now endorsed in many classrooms, she would be recommended to require more explicit Student - Student interaction (McGroarty, 1992). Given the transcripts discussed here, however, a teacher may want to evaluate if such explicit requirements further the stated goal of the class. That is, since these students wanted "to improve their English writing," is that goal met by figuring out how to make students address each other in writing (even if only "in general"), or do they need to learn explicit interpersonal negotiation strategies as well (see Sullivan in this volume for a situation where the latter goal seems predominant)?

4) Requiring student questions. Another teacher technique exemplifies how the CACD environment can be modified for specific cultural groups. Asian students are culturally conditioned to engage in a teacher-dependency cycle. To break that dependency, all of the students in the classes discussed here were required to pose at least two questions for their fellow students during the class hour. In evaluating the CACD system at the end of the semester, a female Chinese speaker reacted in a way that shows her awareness of being forced into something she would probably not have done voluntarily:

> You [the teacher] require everybody to answer what you ask and make two questions to someone else. But if you didn't make us answer your question and make two other questions, I think that you [the teacher] would probably see only one answer and late when class is almost finished.

Such comments reveal that students realize (if not always admit) that the CACD is not a free period for teachers or students. If it fulfills the course goals, a lesson requires thinking and writing from the students and structure and guidance from the teacher. However, the cross-cultural examples just provided suggest that teachers must be flexible enough to allow student freedom without stifling creativity and questioning from the students—and to create conditions for such freedom and questioning in terms that the students will recognize.

IV. Evaluation

Despite its comparative brevity, the research reported on here supports assertions that networking classrooms foster a learner-centered experience, even to the point of reducing some of the negative effects of classroom interactions from cultural background, previous educational practices, and/or gender (Ma, 1996; Sato, 1981; Shackle, 1987). When facilitated in the ways suggested, the Asian freshman international students described here participate fully (defined by US standards), even when previous research has shown that some of these international students do not normally participate in classroom discussions for cultural reasons (Sato, 1981) while others participate minimally due to differential cultural and gender classroom education (Heath, 1992).

The networked computer system seems to empower Asian students to overcome previous cultural training in education and at home by equalizing or balancing the earlier culturally learned behavior—there appears to be a training effect about discourse norms across culture. These students' earlier training, outlined by Heath (1992), taught them to listen and be obedient but not to ask the teacher questions and definitely not to ask other students questions (at least not while the teacher is looking). In an evaluation of the networking system and the class at the end of the semester, one Chinese student wrote: "This system do[es] help me us a lot in participation. Since oriental students are quite shy and reluctant to express themselves. We can express ourselves on the screen in spite of our shyness." This statement bears out the results of the female students' participation in the second InterChange session. Remember that *all* the female students in the second network session (those with Asian backgrounds as well as those from Latin America, the Middle East, and European ones) increased their participation, not just those who were culturally educated to ask questions and discuss assigned readings (Sato, 1981).

While participation within the classroom will always vary by culture and gender, then, even this brief survey of culture and gender variants in a networking environment has clear implications for student-centered pedagogy. To exploit the advantages of this classroom environment, teachers must structure tasks to de-center authority, so everyone becomes a participant—and must structure those tasks in terms that particular students recognize. At the same time, teachers must also maintain networking as a value-neutral tool, through which ideas can be discussed without constant reference to the person originating the idea. That is, exchanges can be used as a forum to negotiate interpersonal differences without the polarization that so often emerges in conventional questions. Moreover, teachers must use the network environment in ways that promote concentration and analysis of writing, and in light of the fact that computer exchanges allow a distinctive form of idea exchange.

While the analyses provided here stress principally the quantity of student participation in writing tasks in a network format, current research indicates that such increases in quantity of writing correlate with student improvement in writing (Briere, 1966; Kepner, 1991; Robb, Ross, & Shortreed, 1986; Semke, 1984; Zamel, 1985). Therefore, at the very least, we as teachers must acknowledge the power of networking in fostering increased output for a large variety of students.

Finally, in order for computers not to go the way of language laboratories, teachers must remember that computers can be used for more than just grammar drills or word processing, and so must investigate exactly what kind of improvements in student achievements they can facilitate. On computer networks, students have the opportunity to practice writing in a meaningful context that they can control to a greater degree than a conventional classroom. Consequently, students are able to practice real language production in ways that can make real differences for their writing style. At the same time, since the teacher can get a complete record of the "discussions" that occur in this classroom, teachers can use this teaching environment to assess their own roles as facilitators of student learning.

Appendix 1—InterChange Record, Fall 1991

50 minute class —8:00 A.M. to 8:50 A. M.

National Origin and Language of Participants

Chinese Speakers	13
Korean Speakers	3
Indonesian Speakers	2
Spanish Speakers	2
Japanese Speaker	1

Appendix 2—InterChange Record, Spring 1992

50 minute class —8:00 A.M. to 8:50 A. M.

National Origin and Language of Participants

Chinese Speakers from Hong Kong and Singapore	12
Chinese Speaker from Malaysia	1
Vietnamese Speaker	1
Spanish Speakers from Mexico, Nicaragua, Peru and Argentina	4
Czech Speaker	1
Arabic Speaker from Lebanon	1

Appendix 3—Comparative Participation by Gender for Fall and Spring Semesters

Number of students	Total Fall Semester	Total Spring Semester
Female	7	6
Male	14	13

Appendix 4—Comparative Line Entries for the Two Fall and Spring Semesters' Transcripts During a Single Class Hour

Message entries coded at between 7-9 words per line

	Fall Semester	Spring Semester
Total line entries by females		
19 lines or more	47	156
11-18 lines	52	16
10 or fewer lines	30	0
Total line entries by males		
19 lines or more	185	126
11-18 lines	70	88
10 or fewer lines	14	19

References

Bellack, A.A., Kliebard, H.M., Hyman, R.T., & Smith Jr., F.L. (1966). *The language of the classroom.* New York: Teachers College Press.

Briere, E. (1966). Quantity before quality in second language composition. *Language Learning, 16*, 141-151.

Brophy, J.E., & Good T.L. (1974). *Teacher-student relationships: Causes and consequences.* NY: Holt, Rinehart and Winston.

Cazden,C.B., John, V.P., & Hymes, D. (Eds.),. (1972). *Functions of language in the classroom.* New York: Teachers College Press.

Chaudron, C. (1988) *Second language classrooms: Research on teaching and learning.* Cambridge: Cambridge University Press.

Chun, D.M. (1994). Using computer networking to facilitate the acquisition of interactive competence. *System, 22*(1), 17-31.

Doughtery, C., & Pica, T. (1986). Information gap tasks: Do they facilitate second language acquisition? *TESOL Quarterly, 20*, 305-325.

Dunkin, M.J., & Biddle, J.B. (1974). *The study of teaching.* NY: Holt, Rinehart and Winston.

Gaies, S. (1983). Learner feedback: An exploratory study of its role in learner feedback. In H.W. Seliger & M.H. Long (Eds.), *Classroom oriented research in second language acquisition.* (pp. 205-217). Rowley, Mass.: Newbury House.

Heath, S.B. (1992). Sociocultural contexts of language development: Implications for the classroom. In P.A. Richard-Amato & M.A. Snow (Eds.), *The multicultural classroom: Readings for content area teachers* (pp.102-125). White Plains, NY: Longman.

Kepner, C.G. (1991). An experiment in the relationship of types of written feedback to the development of second-language writing skills. *The Modern Language Journal, 75*, 305-312.

Kern, R.G. (1995). Restructuring classroom interaction with network computers: Effects on quantity and characteristics of language production. *The Modern Language Journal, 79*, 457-476.

Laosa, L.M. (1979). Inequality in the classroom: Observational research on teacher-student interaction. *Aztlan, 8*, 51-67.

Legaretta, D. (1977). Language choice in bilingual classrooms. *TESOL Quarterly, 11*, 9-16.

Long, M.H., Adams, L., McLean, M., & Castaños, F. (1976). Doing things with words: Verbal interaction in lockstep and small group classroom situations. In J.F. Fanselow & R. Crymes, (Eds.), *On TESOL '76* (pp.137-153). Washington D.C.: TESOL.

Ma, R. (1996). Computer-mediated conversations as a new dimension of intercultural communication between East Asian and North American college students. In Susan C. Herring (Ed.), *Computer-mediated communication: Linguistic, social and cross-cultural perspectives* (pp. 173-185). Philadelphia, PA: Johns Benjamins.

Malcolm X. (1991). Hair. In H. Knepler & M. Knepler (Eds.), *Crossing cultures* (pp. 139-141). New York: Macmillan.

McGroarty, M. (1992). Cooperative learning: The benefits for content-area teachers. In P.A. Richard-Amato & M.A. Snow (Eds.), *The Multicultural classroom: Readings for content area teachers* (pp. 58-70). White Plains, NY: Longman.

Morrison, T. (1991). A slow walk of trees. In H. Knepler & M. Knepler (Eds.), *Crossing cultures* (pp. 67-72). New York: Macmillan.

Peterson, P. L., Wilkinson, L.C., & Hallinan, M.T. (Eds.). (1983). *The Social context of instruction: Group organizations and group processes.* Orlando, Fla. : Academic Press.

Philips, S. (1972). Participation structures and communicative competence: Warm Springs children in community and classroom. In C. Cazden, V.P. John & D.H. Hymes (Eds.), *Functions of language in the classroom*, (pp.370-394). New York: Teachers College Press.

Pica, T., & Doughtery, C. (1985). Input and interaction in the community language classroom: A comparison of teacher-fronted and group activities. In S.M. Glass and C.J. Madden (Eds.), *Input and second language acquisition* (pp. 115-132). Rowley, MA: Newbury House.

Raimes, A. (1991). Out of the woods: Emerging traditions in the teaching of writing. *TESOL Quarterly, 25*, 407-430.

Ramirez, J.D., Yuen, S.D., Ramey, D.R., & Merino, B. (1986). *First year report: longitudinal of immersion programs for language minority children.* Arlington, VA: SRA Technologies.

Robb, T., Ross, S., & Shorthreed I. (1986). Salience of feedback on error and its effect on EFL writing quality. *TESOL Quarterly, 20*, 83-93.

Rulon, K., & McCreary J. (1986). Negotiation of content: Teacher fronted and small group interaction . In R.R. Day. (Ed.), *Talking to learn: Conversation in second language acquisition* (pp. 182-199). Rowley, MA: Newbury House.

Sato, C. (1981). Ethnic styles in classroom discourse. In M. Hines & W. Rutherford (Eds.), *On TESOL '81* (pp. 11-24). Washington DC:TESOL.

Semke, H.D. (1984). Effects of the red pen. *Foreign Language Annals*, 17, 195-202.

Shackle, C. (1987). Speakers of Indian languages. In M. Swan & B. Smith (Eds.), *Learner English* (pp. 170-184). Cambridge: Cambridge University Press.

Smith, B. (1987). Arabic speakers. In M. Swan & B. Smith (Eds.), *Learner English* (pp. 142-157). Cambridge: Cambridge University Press.

Trueba, H.T., Guthrie, G.P., & Hu-Pei Au, K. (Eds.), 1981. *Culture and the bilingual classroom: Studies in classroom ethnography*. Rowley, MA: Newbury House.

Zamel. V. (1985). Responding to student writing. *TESOL Quarterly, 19*, 79-101.

Notes

[1]Complete transcripts of the sessions are available from the author. The Appendices to the present discussion present statistical and demographic breakdowns of the two sessions.

Section III

Motivational Assessments

The two essays in this section, by Beauvois and Jaeglin, explore the efficacy of a computer classroom from a different point of view than that of the earlier studies in this volume. Instead of observing students' behaviors, both researchers turn directly to the students using the computer-assisted classroom, to assess how they assess their motivation and output in this learning environment.

Using information from attitude surveys administered at the start and the close of computer-assisted foreign-language classes, and supplemented by interviews, Beauvois provides data about students' attitudes and self-perception about their classroom behaviors in a networked classroom. Significantly, students' self-reporting closely parallels many of the observations made by researchers: both groups recognize clear advantages in the computer environment for issues like discourse management, monitoring of correctness, and quality and quantity of student production.

Jaeglin approaches the same issues with a different sample in mind to address lingering questions about the perceived utility of computer exchanges at different levels across the foreign language curriculum. Moreover, he compares students' perceptions about computer-assisted classes to those of their instructors. His findings amplify Beauvois' conclusions by suggesting exactly how and when students and instructors would like to use computer-assisted classes, and by presenting some of their concerns and reservations.

E-Talk: Computer-Assisted Classroom Discussion—Attitudes and Motivation

Margaret Healy Beauvois

This chapter explores the affective benefits of real-time computer networking to enhance student communication in the foreign language classroom. In the study described below, the learners responded to pre- and post-study survey instruments and participated in follow-up audio-taped interviews. The efficacy of the local area network (LAN) to encourage use of the target language and to generate positive motivation in students is examined in the context of specific categories developed from the data collected in this descriptive study. The computer-assisted discussions took place in an intermediate French class during a summer session at the University of Texas at Austin, facilitated by the Computers and Writing Research Lab and the English Department.

Objectives of the Study

This study on the use of networked computers to teach French was conducted during four computer-assisted lab sessions in which transcripts of the resulting electronic student exchanges were examined for patterns of discourse as well as for the quantity and quality of student messages. The objective of the study was to explore the nature of classroom communication in a foreign language using a network in class and to identify student response to using computers in second-language learning. As the other research articles in this anthology have focused on analyses of specific linguistic features that emerge in the networking class, this chapter will explore one class's responses to pre- and post-study attitude questionnaires and follow-up audio taped interviews. Therefore, the goals of this chapter include the following:

a) to examine student attitudes toward learning a foreign language on a real-time electronic network,

b) to examine students' relationships to their learning processes, to one another, and to the instructor in the computer classroom, and

c) to identify the linguistic benefits of networking.

Setting and Participants

The course, a third-semester French course taught during the second summer session, was composed of 2 sections for a total of 41 students (20 women and 21 men) ranging in age from 18 to 22, with one 47-year-old. All had successfully completed first- and second-semester French, or equivalent courses. As part of a larger study, all regular classes and all computer sessions were observed during the five-week course.

Both sections used the same text book (*Ensuite: Cours Intermediaire de Français* by Hirsch and Thompson); they shared as a course goal a thorough basic grammar review of French. Both sections were taught by experienced teachers who spoke French a majority of the time in class. The atmosphere in both sections was congenial. Both classes were essentially teacher-centered, although in one class, students occasionally worked in pairs or small groups of three to four students. As part of the course curriculum, the students participated once a week in a 75-minute computer session in which they engaged in the networked discussion (see Appendix I for an example of a typical session). One instructor participated in all four sessions; the other declined to participate in or to attend networked computer sessions.

On the computers, the students exchanged ideas, made comments, and asked questions about the four short texts assigned to be read prior to coming to the session. Each reading was chosen with the specific goal of stimulating student use of the French language, as in the oral classroom discussion. All the texts were considered to be "authentic documents" (i.e., they were written for a French audience as opposed to texts edited for non-native speakers). At the end of each session, two hard copies of all the students' messages were printed out, one synchronous and the other sorted by individual names. In the sorted copies, the instructor targeted and highlighted certain, but not all, errors and returned them to students during the following class period. The students were asked to correct highlighted errors.

The Design of the Study: Attitude Surveys

The research methodology of the study is descriptive, based on analyses of the researcher's field notes augmented by information from pre- and post-study attitudinal questionnaires with follow-up interviews.

On the attitude surveys designed for the purpose, four of the pre-study questions were designed to determine whether computer literacy would be a limiting factor in computer use for the students in the two sections. Since ninety of the students responded that they had used computers in some capacity (from a minimum of 6 months to over 4 years), students' possible lack of computer literacy was not a consideration in this study. Two items were asked on both the pre- and post-study instruments to allow comparison of student attitudes before and after the study. On a 5-point Likert scale (from Strongly Agree to Strongly Disagree) these items were: 1. I am interested in learning French, and 2. I enjoy speaking French in class. The remainder of the pre-study questions illustrated the demographics of the class as described above.

The 21 items in Section 2 of the post-study survey focused on five areas of interest: classroom stress, participation, student perceptions of learning, error correction, and group interaction (see Appendix II for a sample of the survey). These items were designed to examine two areas of student reaction to a networking environment for discussion in a foreign language:

a) student self-assessment of performance in both the classroom and the computer lab;

b) student attitudes specific to the instructional format.

These two areas of inquiry will be examined further in this chapter. To more easily analyze the data, the items Strongly Agree and Agree were grouped together, as were Strongly Disagree and Disagree.

The Post-Study Attitude Questionnaire

The post-study questionnaire was designed to identify not only student attitudes toward use of the networking for communicative exercises, but also the *basis* for those attitudes, that is, their reasons for liking or disliking computer sessions in a foreign language class.

I. Attitudes Toward Stress

Over seventy percent of the forty-one students (based on an average of percentage points of items #5, 10, and 17) agreed that working with a computer was unstressful and facilitated self-expression. These students expressed similar opinions in informal, after-class discussions, as well as in the follow-up interviews conducted to examine further their feelings about the network. The computer lab was described as much less anxiety-producing than the regular classroom.

II. Attitudes Toward Network Participation

The students found the computer experience valuable and enjoyable. Seventy-three percent indicated that they would like to spend more time working in the lab (item # 16). Eighty-eight percent gave a strongly positive response to the idea of using networking for discussions with classmates (item #4), and sixty-eight percent were strongly positive about communicating on network with the instructor (item #9). Eighty-three percent emphasized the social benefits of the computer lab by agreeing strongly or very strongly with "I feel as if I know my classmates better because of the lab sessions" (item # 15).

III. Attitudes Toward Learning

Students were positive regarding their networking time. Ninety percent disagreed with #11 ("I did not learn very much from working on the computer"), no student agreed, and the other ten percent remained neutral. Sixty-three percent strongly felt they had improved their ability to write French (item #12), while seventy-one percent agreed "I improved my ability to read French from working on the computer" (item #14).

On the item dealing with improvement in speaking French (#13), the most common response was neutral (forty-nine percent). In other words, students were unable to say if they improved in oral skills as a result of the four networking experiences. However, in the follow-up interviews, about fifty percent volunteered that they experienced an increase in *confidence* in speaking French as they participated in the network sessions. While it is unclear from these responses in what specific ways computer-assisted discussion affects the skills of reading, writing, and speaking in a networking format, by encouraging language use, it promotes the learners' self-assurance about communicating in the language.

IV. Attitudes Toward Error Correction

Most students (seventy percent—an average of items # 7 and 8) expressed preference (agreed, strongly agreed) for writing without concern for complete grammatical accuracy. Eighty-five percent indicated that it was very helpful to have the printout of their contribution and to have their errors highlighted (item #19). Presumably, delayed error correction (receiving the sorted comments with teacher corrections *after* the session) helped focus student attention on their own errors after the fact, when they were more likely to monitor their expression without the stress of immediate teacher intervention or communicative time constraints.

V. Attitudes Toward Group Interaction

In the early lab sessions, the students expressed some frustration in trying to keep up with the discussion and were overwhelmed by the vast number of entries on the computer screen. When all 20 students in a class are writing simultaneously on the network, messages flash on the screen and scroll by with great rapidity. To deal with this kind of frustration, the instructor divided the class into small groups or "conferences" for two of the four sessions.

Nevertheless, on the post-study survey, when students were asked if they preferred the small group format, only thirty-four percent of the students showed a preference for it (agree, strongly agree). In the follow-up interviews, twenty percent of the students stated that they preferred forming their own small discussion groups on the network as they would naturally in social settings. They claimed that this spontaneous conversational clustering made the electronic discussion more manageable.

Interviews

The purpose of the interviews was to explore in more detail the attitudes identified in the post-study questionnaire. The students were selected from volunteers who expressed willingness to answer questions. Fourteen interviews were chosen for analysis. Eleven of the fourteen interviews were conducted and audio-taped in person, outside of class, on the last day of the session. Three more were conducted and tape-recorded on the telephone during the next week. All participants were asked three general questions based on their questionnaire responses.

I. The Design of the Questions

The goal behind interview questions was to identify learners' views about components of an effective language learning environment. To this end, therefore, the students were asked to comment on the following observations and questions:

1. In oral classroom discussions, when asked to speak only French, the students in your class still tended to slip into English. However, they almost never did this while on the computer network. Did you also notice this? If so, why do you think this happens? Can you offer an explanation of this phenomenon?

2. What effect, if any, do you think the computer network had on the students' discussion? Did students tend to "talk" more or less on the computer? How did they express themselves?

3. What effect do you think the computer had on your ability to read, write, or speak French? Please explain.

The first question probes students' disinclination to code-switch when networking. Students used the target language almost exclusively for the seventy-five minutes of each computer session. During observations of the oral language sessions in these intermediate French classes, however, students frequently engaged in code-switching in posing questions or in asides to one another.

Question two was designed to discover how the students perceived their performance on the network. How did they react to "talking" to their classmates in French by means of the computer? Question three elicits student impressions about how a computer-assisted discussion affected their learning. Since no grades were assigned for networking sessions, the third question addresses student perceptions about how computer work affects their language acquisition within the course curriculum as a whole.

The data collected from the responses to these questions overlapped the boundaries of my original inquiry and for organizational purposes will be grouped into four general categories and twenty-one subsections of those categories. The data collected are defined in Tables I, II, III, and IV and displayed in Figures I, II, III and IV, respectively:

Table 1: Linguistic Benefits

Item	Frequency of Response (Maximum 14)	Percentage of Students
1. Students monitor use of grammar to express themselves	6	42%
2. Students experience increased comprehension	6	42%
3. Students experience increased reading practice	4	28%
4. Students appreciate opportunity for writing practice.	10	71%
5. Students express some transfer of writing skills to speaking	4	28%
6. Students experience increased output	14	100%
7. Students enjoy conversational aspect of electronic interaction	13	92%
8. Students give evidence of automaticity	4	28%

In the category of linguistic benefits, the unanimous student perception of increased use of the target language constituted the most important finding. In the follow-up interviews, the entire group (one hundred percent) mentioned an increase in output over the normal classroom. In fact, the students produced over 200 messages per lab session, with generally several sentences, often complex, per message. Another unanimous student response attributed high output to the fact that they had time to reflect before writing. In the weekly discussion on the network, there were no time constraints on their participation. Students could respond to the instructor's questions at their own pace. Students' comments regarding

FIGURE 1. LINGUISTIC BENEFITS

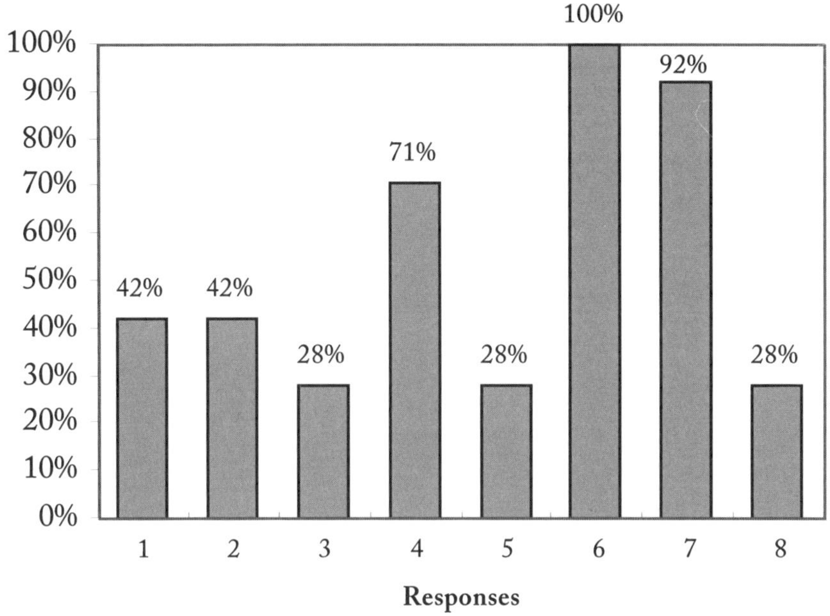

this feature of networking seem to bear out theories that advocate delayed production. This "conversation in slow motion" (Beauvois, 1992b) also reduced the level of anxiety generally associated with oral production (Young, 1990).

Time was also mentioned by forty-two percent of the students in connection with code switching and grammatical accuracy. When asked why they used French rather than English in their networking exchanges, students explained that they were able to take the time to monitor their use of grammar to better express their ideas:

- "In the lab, we do have our books there and . . . you can take the time to look up a word."
- "We had time to form our conversations. We could sit there and think."
- "You can find a way around . . . so you can say it in French."
- "You have time . . . to think about how to conjugate the verb."

The freedom from having to produce target language in some one else's time frame seemed to release the students to create meaningful, playful and more accurate conversations with their classmates and instructor.

Cumulatively, such individual benefits probably account for the positive student attitude (ninety-two percent) toward the conversational aspect of electronic communication and to their feeling of control over their output. If communicative competence in language acquisition occurs "when the learner has the chance to negotiate meaning in unplanned discourse" (Ellis, 1984), then the network experience conforms ideally to that criteria. In commenting on the quality as well as the quantity of the discourse, one student said: "We [spoke] more and on a deeper level on InterChange [the software package used] than in the class." Another student expressed it this way: "It actually helps in a conversation with your instructor . . . it's not a drill and response where my role is just to sort of respond with the correct answer. . . . So it makes for real conversation." Another one pointed out: "I didn't necessarily answer the teacher right out. I thought that was a big plus!" And in a similar vein: " I said more things on the computer than I can say in the classroom, because the classroom dynamic is that he [the teacher] has to teach and we have to listen." Research done in English composition classes (as well as the results reported by Sullivan above) suggests a similar type of discourse in which we see "dialogue whose . . . honesty I have yet to encounter in a verbal class discussion, especially from students who ordinarily will not volunteer opinions in a conventional classroom setting" (Peterson, as cited in Bump, 1990).

Another recurring theme dealt with the monitoring options available during network exchanges. For forty-two percent of the students, the monitoring of language form was very important . As one student said, "I would go back and change the spelling, you know, O.K. but that's just me." Others mentioned having time to review verb conjugations or to look up vocabulary words. A very small percentage (two percent) expressed a desire to use accent marks, a grammatical form we did not observe on the network. The students who did specifically monitor their output were not at the same time inhibited from participating in the on-going conversation, an effect often observed in oral discourse when students do not speak for fear of making errors. In fact, as was stated above and confirmed repeatedly by other studies, there was not less but rather more participation from the whole class than in the regular classroom (over 200 "utterances" per session).

Other benefits documented include perceptions of increased reading and comprehension: "When I read something someone has written I am able to fill in the blanks a little better. . . . I can still make it through the context. I find it harder to do that in the classroom," and "[i]t helped me just to understand what we were studying in the class, ... [and to follow] what the readings were about." Another student enthusiastically expressed this reaction: "You have to read what everybody says . . . and it helps to be able to go back and look at how they placed things," and "I mean you're sitting there reading the whole time! . . . You're learning the vocabulary and structures."

Seventy-one percent expressed the need for writing: "Some people did sort of read more than they wrote, but I tried to write as much as I could," and "the InterChange helped me with the writing. There was not nearly enough writing in the [regular] class." Other students identified the already established advantages of word processing in this real-time, synchronous environment: "I can't think of a way to say what I want to say and there is no way to go back . . . When you're writing it, you go 'oop' and you back space . . . and you're out of your trap." While there is no intent here to diminish the importance of oral practice in language learning, it is important to attend to student-expressed needs for more attention to developing writing skills as they correlate with accuracy in such production.

Some students (twenty-eight percent) identified a link between written and oral skills on the network: "I think it improved my conversation somewhat because it quickened my responses and my thinking. I would just write as if I was speaking," and ". . . you would write, speaking in your brain." Another twenty-eight percent made references to their experience of automaticity (McLaughlin, 1987) as a linguistic benefit. Statements such as "We really used what we learned in class" and "In an InterChange it was so conversational, I felt as if I were re-using the things I already had at my fingertips." One student was concerned that there might be "less improvement," presumably in accurate language use or acquisition of new knowledge, than was the case in the oral classroom.

Improvement can, of course, be packaged in many guises. In his "hierarchical task structure of speaking," McLaughlin describes improvement in speaking as occurring when "a component of the task becomes automatized," thereby freeing the learner to focus on more difficult tasks to accomplish (McLaughlin, 1987, p. 136). Students' comments about networking showed an awareness that some of their communication in French on the network demanded little of the "processing energy" McLaughlin refers to (p.134). In other words, networking helps to routinize certain skills of expression. Lack of stress and extensive practice allows students to develop automatic structures.

Table 2. Affective Benefits

1. Students feel less stress than in the classroom	13	92%
2. Students have adequate time to think and compose messages	14	100%
3. Students feel empowered to control the conversational task	13	92%
4. Everyone always has a turn	13	92%
5. Students experience greater ease of communication	13	92%
6. The network allows for individual learning styles	10	71%
7. Students express a positive reaction and claim to enjoy the experience	14	100%

FIGURE 2. AFFECTIVE BENEFITS

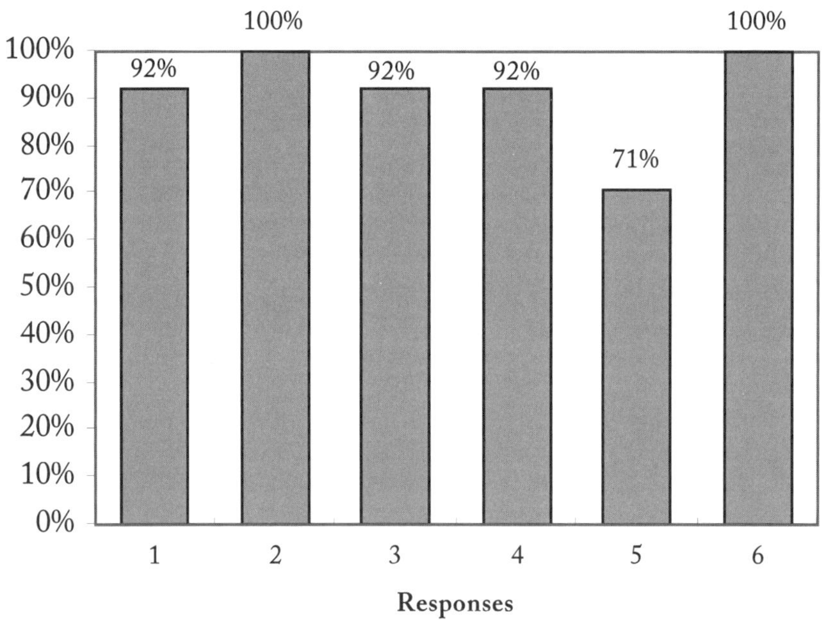

Affective Benefits

As Table 2 and Figure 2 indicate, ninety-two percent of the students interviewed cited the low stress atmosphere of the network lab as their reason for using the target language. They explained that in the classroom "you're kinda on the spot" with "twenty people waiting for your response and the instructor is standing right in front of you," and you "get so scared" that you "just speak English to get it right." In the lab, however, "no one is waiting for your answer." All fourteen students interviewed (one hundred percent) stated that they were able to use French to communicate because there was, once again, *time* to process, and it was therefore "easier for me to think," "there was less pressure, less stress, for a quick answer," thereby lowering the affective filter. In one sense, these students' words may be telling us more about what is wrong with the regular classroom than what is right with the electronic medium. By their own statements, they confirm theories that cite performance anxiety in the classroom as an impediment to freedom of expression (Young, 1990, 1991).

Some students did mention "a little stress trying to keep up with what was going on" and that they would "have to hurry" to keep up with the on-going conversation. Still, this could be considered beneficial rather than debilitating stress, as it seemed to enforce the student's sense that they need to read and respond quickly rather than to inhibit the student's attention and production.

One interesting issue identified by ninety-two percent of the students was the experience of freedom from forced responses. On the network, students felt in control of the conversation. "You're not forced to say anything immediately," "... no one was waiting for you to speak," and "you do get your chance to speak, you do get your turn, because there is always a turn. You don't have to wait for someone to finish theirs." Related to their perception of having more opportunities to initiate communication, students also saw an altered relationship with instructor input in a computer classroom. "I answered you [the instructor] because ... something you said appealed to me, not because you were the teacher." Indeed, a new level of openness in interpersonal dealings, as previously reported (Peterson, 1989), was also identified: "I disagreed with him [the teacher] once or twice or I agreed with him once or twice—there is actually a conversation going on ..." The perceived lack of teacher-driven discussion resulted in a different class focus than the one characteristic of oral classrooms. As one student put it, "[i]n the [computer] lab ... the center of attention is the discussion with students. In the classroom the center of attention is the teacher."

In addition, the students were exposed to much comprehensible input in the form of each others' interlanguage. They developed their own sort of "foreigner language" (Ferguson, 1975) by asking questions, simplifying their "utterances," and re-phrasing so as to "express myself in a way that people can understand." Once again in keeping with the tenets of recent second-language learning theories, students were negotiating for meaning within their own discourse community.

One student told of his control of the conversation by forming his own small group to make the discussion more manageable. He described it this way: "Whoever I got messages from first . . . I'd pretty much stay with them and I wouldn't like really talk to anyone other than those like about four people." In fact, he had spontaneously formed a cooperative learning group without benefit of teacher intervention. The advantages of small groups for discussion is well known in the educational research community (Johnson, & Johnson 1987; Slavin, 1989). This innate need for a sense of community leads us to the next topic, that of student perception of interpersonal benefits.

Table 3. Interpersonal Benefits

1. Students get to know classmates better	13	92%
2. Students experience opportunities for "real" conversation on the LAN	6	42%
3. Male students are perceived as less "macho", more sensitive, more talkative	8	57%

Figure 3. Interpersonal Benefits

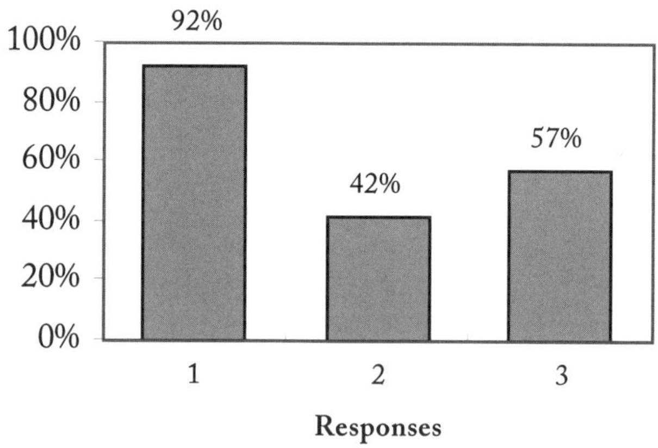

Interpersonal Benefits

In monitoring each others' participation and performance, all the students mentioned a different atmosphere present in the lab environment, as the table above confirms: "Certain people came out in the lab, whereas in the class they would have been more restrained and restricted." They also noticed a definite change in their classmates' discourse: " They talk about all kinds of stuff on the computer and . . . in class they just don't say it." The students' perception of a "deeper" level of communication, as mentioned above, allowed for more openness of communication. "If you sit around with people for an hour and a half which is in essence what was happening in the lab, you get to know them, better. I think there is a sort of superficialness and reluctance in class."

The benefits to the reserved or shy student found in Bump's research (1990) were also mentioned: "Whatever their personality was it became even more so in the lab" and "Some people . . . are just generally shy and don't speak out, but when you're on the computer it doesn't really matter." These advantages to students "marginalized" in the normal routine of classroom discussion were also found to be true in previous research in the area of English literature and composition courses, and was observed in the ESL classes held in the computer lab (Bump, 1990; Faigley, 1990; Markley, 1991). Unlike the findings in these English classes, where men are shown to dominate classroom discussion and females are more reticent to speak, in this foreign language study, males were described (by the men and women in the class) as talking less in the classroom, as showing their "sensitive side," and as being "very talkative" on the computer. One student added this perception: "Maybe especially for the guys, the screen allows them not to be so macho."

Meaningful conversation led to a greater knowledge of class members and established a willingness to risk. As one student said: "I got to know my classmates better and that made me more willing to make mistakes." The awareness of a certain security that existed within the social context of networked discourse seems to uphold theories advanced by Vygotsky and others about language learning being essentially a social phenomenon. The "zone of proximal development" (Vygotsky, 1962) was experienced, if not identified as such, by students talking about participation on the network: "I was able to pick things up from the better students." They also expressed the importance of "scaffolding"—in going back and looking at "what other people had written" as well as waiting "until other people answered and then build on theirs." This concept of learners bridging the gap of oral proficiency for one another is perhaps only possible in an electronic medium in which the conversation is held in abeyance to be studied by the interlocutors as they continue to converse with one another. The implications for second language research in this area are enormous.

The kind of group support and bonding described by the students has been shown to enhance students' self-esteem and motivation for learning (Johnson, & Johnson, 1987). The idea that they would have "felt a lot worse about missing an InterChange session than about missing a regular class" was expressed informally by several students during the course of this summer session as well as in semester-long courses (Kelm, 1992). It is safe to say, I think, that the students participating in this study experienced the positive effect of belonging to a community of speakers of a foreign language and the pride of producing together coherent, readable documents in that foreign language, thus creating a new sense of the classroom discourse community.

Table 4. Perceived Computer Control of French Language Output

1. Students perceive existence of "rules" for exclusive use of French	12	86%
2. Students feel compelled to participate on the network	14	100%
3. Students observe that English is almost never used on the network.	14	100%

Figure 4. Perceived computer control of French Language Output

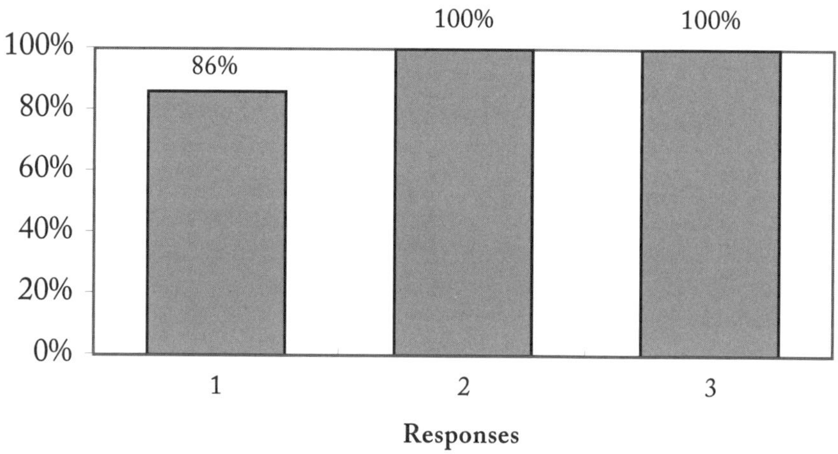

Perceived Computer Control of French Language Output

The final item identified by a large majority of students (eighty-six percent) was an interesting perception of certain "rules" for behavior in the lab. Although such "rules" were never stated by the instructor, the students intuitively felt they were "clearly established" and that they governed the computer discussion in the following ways: only French was to be used on the computer and everyone was expected to participate in the discussion. There were several references to the fact that they, the students, "had" to participate, "had to speak French," and felt "some pressure to type in French," although no such obligation was perceived in the regular classroom where the instructors frequently stated that the students must speak French. One student even felt that it would have been "cheating" to use English in the lab. It could be that the print on the screen had the focusing power to keep the students in the target language, or perhaps it was the absence of distractions in the computer lab. Further research will be needed to elucidate this interesting perception of the compelling computer control over use of the target language.

As an extension of this perception, one student expressed the idea that the computer is "really your mode to discuss extracurricular things... Even if you're talking about what this person had to drink last week-end, it's still in French. We were always taking in French!" The astonishment evident in this student's comment indicates that the target language is not always seen as a means of communication but rather too often as an academic endeavor in which one memorizes certain grammatical forms and learns a number of vocabulary words. The classroom is not perceived as the place for "real" conversation (i.e., what *they* want to talk about). Students perceived network conversation to be more realistic perhaps because it allowed them the freedom to control their output.

Conclusion

Computer-assisted discussion presents an entirely new way of looking at classroom communication in a foreign language. It changes the whole discussion process by allowing for a moderation of ideas, phrasing and re-phrasing of thoughts beforc expressing them. The student does not experience the feeling of being "stuck," but rather is able to decide to change just one word or a phrase and get out of the verbal interaction "box" s/he feels trapped in.

Research done on the effects of classroom anxiety on language learning suggests that students' verbal interaction in front of the class is the most anxiety-producing activity encountered in the language classroom (Young, 1990). Discussions held in the computer lab seem to have the opposite effect on the learners. Over and over, students comment on the almost stress-free atmosphere experienced on the network. In addition, electronic discourse allows for attention to individual learning styles. As documented by student comments stated above, the individual differences of the learners were accommodated by the network process, as they respond in their own way, in their own time.

The monitoring of one's oral production and one's written discussion differs fundamentally. Electronic discourse encourages the "speaker" to do a more thorough job of repair both at the time of the "utterance" and later as well when the sorted individual student comments can be studied in depth. This characteristic of "thinking made visible" (Sills, 1990) is unique to the computer environment. One has the possibility, as in no other setting, to form a conversation, to check it at the time of production, and then to review it a day or so later.

The polylogue generated by networking seems to provide the "dynamic exchange" described by Savignon who emphasizes *negotiation* as the means to attaining communicative competence in a foreign language (1972, 1983). By providing opportunities for students to function in the language in social interactions, communication on the network contributes to their ability to initiate conversations, respond at will, take turns, and carry on meaningful conversation in the target language. Students recognized in their interviews that in the regular classroom in spoken discourse, they would more readily use English to express themselves if unable to think of an appropriate expression in French. Additional time for reflection apparently enables students to engage in less code-switching in computer discussions than would be the case in an oral classroom.

Based on the positive affect reported by the students in this study, it can be said that networking was an effective motivating environment. The students' reports ranged from enjoyment of the experience to expressions of strong enthusiasm for this method of student-to-student and student-to- teacher talk. The time to think, the lack of pressure, and the permanent nature of the discussion allowing for subsequent error correction were the most frequent advantages cited.

Another important finding in this study of computer-assisted communication in a second language is that it is essentially a student-centered activity. We have known for some time that teachers tend to dominate classroom conversation; that they do sixty percent of the talking (Bellack, Kliebard, Hyman, & Smith, 1966; Dunkin, & Biddle, 1974). On the network, the instructors' role must change as they become participants in the discussion; facilitators rather than controllers. Such findings do not suggest a superiority of instruction or learning in the lab over oral practice in the classroom. However, the results do seem to suggest that this particular use of computer-assistance in the teaching of language integrates well into the foreign language curriculum.

Appendix I: Computer-Assisted Discussion Sample

What follows is a printout of a small part of a lab session. Only the names of the students involved have been changed. The synchronous messages are numbered in order of their appearance on the computer screen and are preceded by the sender's name.

1 -Peggy Beauvois:
Bonjour tout le monde! Nous allons discuter le texte "La Kid Generation." Voila quelques questions pour commencer notre "conversation." Vous pouvez repondre a toutes les questions, ou poser vos propres questions, comme vous voulez.

1 Peggy Beauvois
Hello everyone! We are going to discuss the text "The Kid Generation." Here are a few questions to begin our "conversation." You can answer all the questions or ask your own questions, as you like.

A. Quelles sont les idees que vous avez trouvees les plus frappantes ou interessantes dans le texte? Qu'est-ce que vous en pensez, vous-meme?

A. Which ideas did you think were the most striking or interesting in the text? What do you think about them, yourselves?

B. Etes-vous d'accord avec la premiere phrase du texte: "Il n'y a plus de jeunesse?" Pourquoi oui, ou pourquoi non?

B. Do you agree with the first sentence of the text: "There is no more youth?" Why yes or no?

C. Y a-t-il des phrases ou des mots que vous ne comprenez pas? Lesquels?

C. Are there sentences or words that you don't know? Which ones?

D. Comment etiez-vous a l'age de 15-16 ans? Est-ce que votre opinion comptait beaucoup dans les decisions de votre famille? Vous entendiez-vous bien avec vos parents, vos freres et soeurs?
****

D. What were you like at age 15 - 16? Did your opinion count a lot in the decisions of your family? Did you get along with your parents, your brothers and sisters?
****

2 Bob Cole:	2. Bob Cole:
3 Bob Cole: C' est difficile n' est pas?	3 Bob Cole: This is difficult, isn' t it?
4 Mary Lewis: A l' age de 15-16 ans, j' etais tres timide avec mon pere parce qu' il etait tres severe et il faisait toutes les decisions dans la famille.	4. Mary Lewis: At 15-16 years old, I was very shy with my father because he was very strict and he made all the decisions in the family.
5 Kevin Clark: Bob. . . . . Quand vous avait 16 ans, jouait-vous des sportes? Je jouait le football, mais ne pas le football americain ... le football "soccer." Et vous? Au revoir. Kevin	5. Kevin Clark: Bob....When you was 16, did you play sports? I played football, but not american football...."soccer" football. And you? Good-bye. Kevin.
6 Lena Portman: Mon famille est tres vieillesse. Les enfants ont tres petite opinion dans les decisions.	6. Lena Portman: My family is very old fashioned. The children have a very small opinion in the decisions.
7 Lena Portman: Bob C' est tres difficile.	7. Lena Portman: Bob It is very difficult.
8 Peggy Beauvois: Marie, vous dites que votre pere prenait toutes les decision dans votre famille; est-ce que votre mere etait d' accord avec lui?	8. Peggy Beauvois: Mary, you say that your father made all the decisions in your family; did your mother always agree with him?
9 Kyle Parsons: Lena, quand j' avais 15 ans, je n' ai choisi en la voiture de ma famille, ou la maison de ma famille. Mais, j' avais beaucoup des decisions de mes vetements, mes amis, etc	9. Kyle Parsons: Lena, when I was 15, I did not choose my family' s car, or house. But I had lots of decisions about my clothes, my friends, etc.

10 Carl Brown: aujourd'hui, les enfants n'aiment pas lire. Beaucoup d'enfants sont stupides. Au lieu, ils aiment l'argent. Malheureusement, d'argent a intoxique leurs pensees.	10 Carl Brown: today, kids do not like to read. Lots of kids are stupid. Instead, they like money. Unfortunately, money intoxicates their thoughts.
11 Peggy Beauvois: Bob, que vous etes courageux! Le premier a ecrire un message! BRAVO!	11. Peggy Beauvois: Bob, you are brave! The first one to write a message! BRAVO!
12 Sam Cullum: Les idees que je trouve les plus interessantes sont eux de la publicite. Ce sont tres dangereux.	12 Sam Cullum: The ideas that I find the most interesting are the ones about advertising. They are very dangerous.

Appendix II: Poststudy Instrument : SECTION 2

In this section, please indicate whether you agree or disagree with some statements about second language learning environments and about the InterChange lessons in the computer lab.

Instructions: Mark your answers on the line provided.

A	B	C	D	E
Strongly Agree	Agree	Neutral	Disagree	Strongly Disagree

1. I enjoy using computers to learn new material. _______
2. I prefer learning a foreign language from an instructor in a classroom. _______
3. I participate more when we write on the computer network than when we discuss in class. _______
4. I enjoyed discussing texts with my classmates on the computer. _______
5. I was able to express myself easily on the computer. _______
6. I prefer oral discussion of texts in class. _______
7. I liked not having to worry about typographic mistakes. _______
8. I liked having the opportunity to communicate without paying special attention to grammar. _______
9. I like this method of communication with my instructor. _______
10. I felt intimidated when expressing my ideas. _______
11. I did not learn very much from working on the computer. _______
12. I have improved my ability to write French because of the lab sessions. _______
13. I have improved my ability to speak French because of the lab sessions. _______
14. I have improved my ability to read French because of the lab sessions. _______
15. I feel as if I know my classmates better because of the lab sessions. _______
16. I would have liked to spend more time working in the lab. _______
17. I felt stress while working in the lab. _______
18. I prefer writing in French in my own, not in the lab. _______
19. I found it helpful to have the printed copy of my own messages for grammar correction. _______
20. I like using pseudonyms. _______
21. I prefer whole class discussions, as opposed to smaller conferences.

References

Batson, T. (1988). The ENFI project: A networked classroom approach to writing instruction. *Academic Computing, 2*(5), 32-33.

Beauvois, M. H. (1992a) *Computer-assisted classroom discussion in French using networked computers.* Unpublished doctoral dissertation, the University of Texas at Austin.

Beauvois, M. H. (1992b). Computer-assisted discussion in the foreign language classroom: Conversation in slow motion. *Foreign Language Annals, 25*, 1992.

Bellack, A. A., Kliebard, H.M., Hyman, R.T., & Smith, F.L., Jr. (1966). *The language of the classroom.* New York: Teachers College Press.

Bump, J. (1990). Radical changes in class discussion using networked computers. *Computers and the Humanities, 24*, 49-65.

Carter, L. (1989, March). *Telecommunications and networked personal computers: Opening up the classroom.* Paper presented at the Conference on College Composition and Communication, Seattle.

Dunkin, M.J., & Biddle, B.J. (1974). *The study of teaching.* New York: Holt, Rinehart & Winston.

Ellis, R. (1984). *Classroom second language development.* Oxford: Pergammon Press.

Faigley, L. (1990). Subverting the electronic workbook: Teaching writing using networked computers. In D. Daiker and M. Morenberg (Eds.), *The writing teacher as researcher: Essays in the theory of class-based writing* (pp. 290-312). Portsmouth, NH: Heineman.

Faigley, L., Cherry, R. D., Joliffe, D.A., & Skinner, A. (1985). *Assessing writers' knowledge and processes of composition* (pp. 90-91). Ablex: Norwood, NJ.

Ferguson, C. (1975). Towards a characterization of English foreigner talk. *Anthropological Linguisitics, 17*, 1-14.

Johnson, D., & Johnson, R. (1987) *Learning together and alone*, Englewood Cliffs, NJ: Prentice-Hall. Second Edition.

Kelm, O. R. (1992). The use of synchronous computer networks in second language instruction: A preliminary report. *Foreign Language Annals, 25*, 5, 441-454.

Kinneavy, J.L. (1991, March). *I won't teach again without computers.* Paper presented at the Conference on College Communication and Composition. Boston.

Markley, P. (1991). Creating independent ESL writers and thinkers: A look at a computer network designed for composition. (article submitted for publication)

McLaughlin, B.(1987). *Theories of second languge learning.* London: Edward Arnold.

Peterson, N. (1989). The Sounds of silence: Listening for difference in the computer-networked collaborative writing classroom. In T.W. Batson (Ed.) *Proposal abstracts from the 5th computers and writing conference, University of Minnesota, Minneapolis, May 12-14.* Washington, DC: Gallaudet University: 6-8.

Savignon, S.J. (1972). *Communicative compentence*: An experiment in foreign language teaching. Philadelphia: Center for Curriculum Development.

Savignon, S.J. (1983). *Communicative competence: Theory and classroom practice.* Reading, MA: Addison-Wesley.

Savignon, S.J. (1991). Research on the role of communication in classroom-based foreign language acquisition: On the interpretation, expression and negotiation of meaning. In B. Freed (Ed). *Second language acquisition research and the classroom.* Lexington, MA: D.C. Heath.

Sills, C. (1990). Monmouth college: Developing effective pedagogy for computer-enhanced writing instruction. *College Microcomputer, 8* (4).

Slatin, J. (1991). Is there a class in this text? Creating knowledge in the electronic classroom. In Edward Barrett (Ed.), *Sociomedia: Multimedia, hypermedia, and the social construction of knowledge* (pp. 27-51). Cambridge, MA: MIT Press.

Slavin, R. E. (1989). Cooperative learning and student achievement . In R. E. Slavin (Ed.), *School and classroom orgainzation.* Hillsdale, NJ: Erlbaum.

Taylor, P. (1989, March). The authority of readers and writers in computer-based dialogue. Paper presented at the Conference on College Communication and Composition. Seattle, WA.

Underwood, J. (1984). *Linguistics , computers and the language teacher: A communicative approach.* Rowley, MA: Newbury House.

Underwood, J. (1987). Correo: Electronic mail as communicative practice. Computers in research and teaching, *Hispania, 70.*

VanPatten, B. (1991). The foreign language classroom as a place to communicate. In B. Freed (Ed.), *Foreign language acquisition research and the classroom.* Lexingon, MA: D. C. Heath.

Vygotsky, L. (1962). *Thought and language.* Cambridge, MA: MIT Press.

Young, D. J. (1990). An investigation of student's perspectives on anxiety and speaking. *Foreign Language Annals, 23* (6): 539-553.

Learners' and Instructors' Attitudes Towards Computer-Assisted Class Discussion

Christophe Jaeglin

Networked computers, allowing classes to participate in a closed circuit "e-mail" discussion on a local area network, have recently emerged as a significant teaching tool at both the secondary and post-secondary level (Brierley, & Kemble, 1991; Dunkel, 1990; Kelm, 1992). Some network programs have been designed to offer particular advantages for foreign language and English composition classes (Beauvois, 1992; Bender, 1993; Chun [this volume]; Kemp, 1993). Underlying these applications is the presumption that foreign language writing is as much a process as is writing in the native language (Barnett, 1989). If so, opportunities for peer and teacher clarification of feedback on writing may prove more helpful to the foreign language writer than feedback that is unilateral between teacher and student (Cohen, 1991). This paper reports on a survey of student perceptions about the ease and value of using networking as a facet of their course work, in an effort to ascertain whether the benefits and attitude shifts documented for English composition (e.g., Bump, 1990) are experienced by foreign language learners as well.

A survey of fifty-four students from seven foreign language classes and their instructors was developed to compare the attitudes of learners and instructors towards Computer-Assisted Class Discussion (CACD). The goals of the present analysis are two. The first seeks to establish students' evaluation of CACD across the curriculum (not only within a single class, but across various levels, and as reflecting differing instructional styles). To accomplish this goal, the survey analyzed results from participating classes from three different languages (Spanish, Portuguese, and German) and at different levels of instruction ranging from first-year to upper division (sixth semester) college levels, to see if, taken as a whole, opinions of these groups would differ when compared with single teacher surveys, such as that of Beauvois (1992). The second goal is to identify areas in which student perceptions about the value and use of CACD were congruent or at variance with attitudes of their instructors—that is, to see if there was any overt difference in learning styles and expectations between the two groups.

Since foreign language attitude research on CACD has, to this point, generally been undertaken by one teacher with his or her students, the sample in other studies has been small (under fifteen students), and only a particular level/semester and language have been assessed (Beauvois, 1992; Kelm, 1992). Would the positive affective findings cited by Beauvois be reproduced in a more diverse student population? In conjunction with views solicited from different foreign languages and class levels, the questionnaire explored specific types of perceptions. One set of perceptions revolved around skill transfer—the extent to which students and their teachers saw their writing on the CACD as interchangeable with or informing their classwork in listening, reading, or speaking. A second set of questions asked participants whether, in their perceptions, optimal levels for CACD existed. Third, questions solicited views of students and teachers as regards CACD use overall, as well as at a particular learning level.

The Questionnaire

Learners and instructors responded to an in-house questionnaire developed to address the questions above and to see whether teacher and student views on these questions would differ among groups surveyed. The questionnaire consisted of a total of thirty-seven questions (See Appendix A).[1] The first twenty-three questions asked participants to use a five-point Likert scale (Strongly Agree to Strongly Disagree) to describe their experiences with the particular software used. The last five questions on the student questionnaire were open-ended, designed to elicit opinions in student language. Questions 24-32, filled out only by the instructors, were multiple-choice items designed to correspond with student questions, but from a teachers' perspective. In the actual survey process, most questionnaires were filled out in the computer laboratory, although a few students and teachers chose to complete them outside of class.

Setting and Participants

With the exception of four thirty- to forty-year old learners in the sample, all of the fifty-four foreign language students who participated (from the Department of Germanic Languages and the Department of Spanish and Portuguese) were between nineteen and twenty-three years old. Gender distribution in all classes was between forty to sixty percent. Two of the seven participating classes were composed of first-year language students, four were second-year classes, and one was an upper-division course.

This unequal distribution in level among participants resulted because we were unable to obtain more upper-division language students who were working on a LAN, since computer sessions in our institution are still rare at this level of instruction. Similarly, first-year instructors, most of whom are graduate assistants at this university, tend to be bound to a very full, prescribed syllabus and are reluctant to devote session to activities considered extraneous to their program. A further caveat was upheld: in order to preserve the impartiality of the results, neither the author nor his thesis advisor participated in the survey, leaving the instructor count short even though seven instructors actually taught the seven classes assessed.

The computer sessions in these classes were held mainly on Mondays or Fridays in a media classroom where twenty Macintosh Computers are set-up in an S-shape and networked through AppleTalk, using Daedalus InterChange software, as described earlier in this volume.[2] The InterChange sessions lasted approximately fifty minutes in all the classes. Within this common framework, however, formats for the various classes differed. Some instructors had students engage in e-mail-style conversations involving the class as a whole. Others encouraged "conferencing": that is, setting up e-mail exchanges limited to a group of students within the class.

Not only groupings, but assigned tasks differed between classes, as well. However, most teachers asked students to address specific issues and use grammar or vocabulary taught in regular class sessions. Some varied formats from week to week—assigning commentary in regard to particular readings or video viewing assignments, for example, or suggesting a particular discursive approach to steer production (such as arguing for or against, persuading someone to adopt, or rejecting a particular point of view).

The students exert a significant degree of control over their production in this environment. To open the software program, the user clicks on the Daedalus icon on the otherwise empty screen. As illustrated, the main window (see Figure 1 below) occupies the largest part of the screen. From a menu bar, the user can choose InterChange (or one of the other features described above, such as the "conferencing" option). If students select InterChange, a chart will be displayed from which they can choose their course and their names.[3] After typing in her password, the student has now successfully "logged in" to her class session. If the instructor has not posted any assignment, the program will display two empty windows. If the instructor has posted an assignment in advance (by selecting "Post Assignment" from the Utilities Menu), that assignment will appear in the main window at the top of the screen.

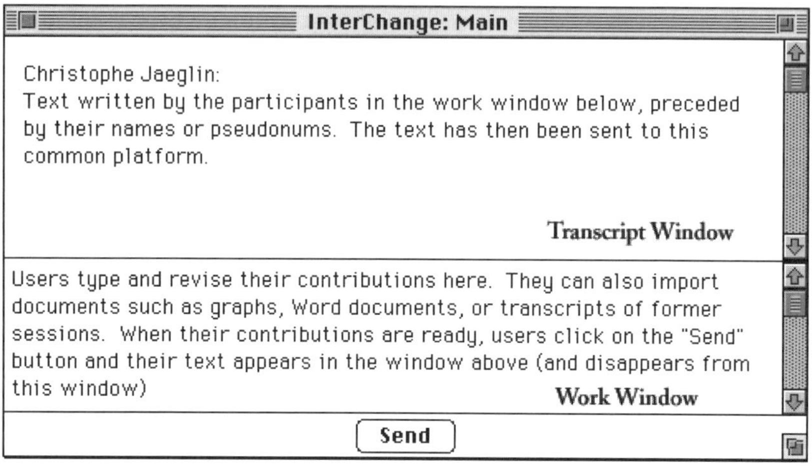

FIGURE 1. A DAEDALUS INTERCHANGE SCREEN

The screen is divided into two parts: the upper part (main window) is common for all users. All messages sent throughout the course of the class hour are available when users scroll up and down the screen, which they can do by using the arrows on the right hand side of the window. The lower part of the screen, or work window, is a personal writing space. Users type their text in the lower, work window and can then revise it before sending it to the community or "main" window.

When students are satisfied with the text they have produced in the work window, they need only click on the "Send" button (lower mid-section of the window) in order to transfer their text to the main window, where it can be read by all the participants, including themselves. The fact that users can scroll up and down within the main windows allows them to "catch up" on comments they may have missed while composing, or to check on whether a message has been accurately understood. In effect, these functions enable students to write in direct response to what they have read.

As was true of tasks assigned, feedback procedures from these sessions depended on individual teachers. Frequently, transcripts were handed back to students to read and assess their performance in class with respect to either the substance of their texts or language use.[4] Although no one reported having graded these transcripts for language accuracy, evaluative policies based on InterChange performance varied among teachers: two teachers used transcripts to assign grades (based on clarity or use of assigned vocabulary); others gave credit for numbers of entries; others gave credit for attendance *per se*.

Findings

As already noted, the questionnaire was designed to compare responses about two general areas: 1) whether teachers and students view the CACD as a narrow learning tool, fostering only writing practice, and 2) whether the particular program used (the Daedalus InterChange) or the level at which it was used posed special problems or benefits. To assess whether participants saw a potential skills transfer from writing on this network to listening or speaking, two questions expressly asked students and teachers to compare the "learning opportunity" for speaking, or listening activity in their "regular class" with language use during computer sessions (questions 11 and 12 for students, 28 and 29 for teachers). The questions comparing reading and writing asked students and teachers whether, in their opinion, computer exchange give "more practice" (questions 9 and 10 for students, 26 and 27 for teachers). Since little or no speaking or listening normally occurs during a CACD class (or since what does occur is clearly not the class focus), this distinction in formulation of questions about skill transfer ("similar learning opportunity" versus "more practice") was deemed critical.

As would be expected, the majority of students and teachers agreed that InterChange gives more practice in writing than a conventional FL course: 75.9% of the students and 80% (four out of five) of the teachers (see Figure 2) answered affirmatively to the question: "When compared with a regular class I find computer InterChange gives me more practice in writing." As with the charts that follow, unless otherwise specified, the

Figure 2. Writing practice with InterChange

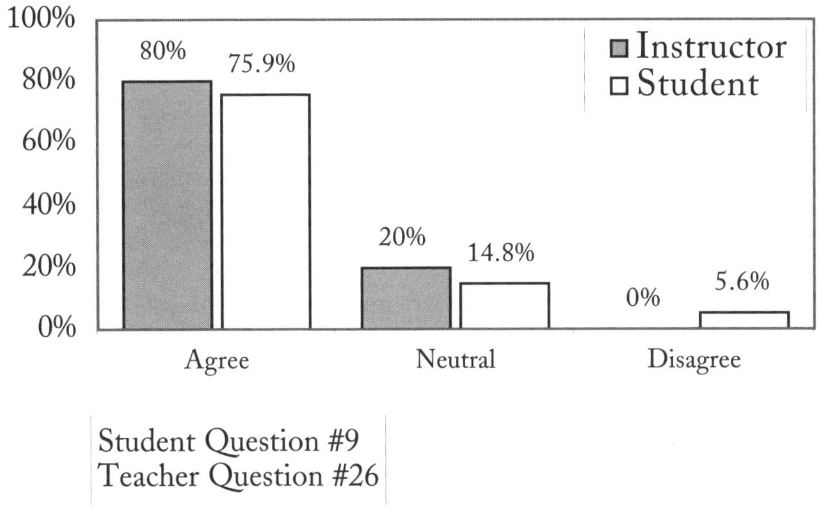

included graphs coalesce both the "strongly agree" and "agree" and the "disagree" and "strongly disagree" categories.

When asked about the amount of reading students would get through InterChange, however, the student and teacher groups responded differently (see Figure 3). A majority of students (50%) responded affirmatively to the assertion: "When compared with a regular classroom I find the computer InterChange gives me more practice in reading," whereas a third of them answered this question in a neutral way. The teachers responded affirmatively by 60% (three out of five) and negatively by 40% to the assertion: "When compared with a regular classroom I find a computer InterChange gives my students more practice in reading."

Figure 3. Reading practice with InterChange

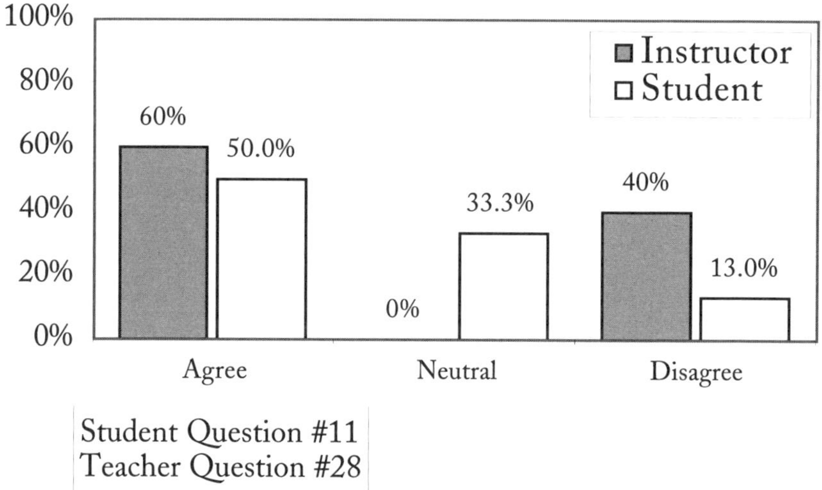

With regard to listening, all participants (see Appendix A, student question 11 and teacher question 28) indicated that a traditional course offered more practice than an InterChange session, not a surprising finding, given the general absence of listening opportunities. It was therefore striking to note that, with regard to speaking and the InterChange experience, teachers and students differed somewhat in their views, with 24% of all students (13 of 54) perceiving a similarity between computer exchanges and speaking whereas none of their teachers did, as shown in Figure 4:

Figure 4. Speaking communicatively in InterChange

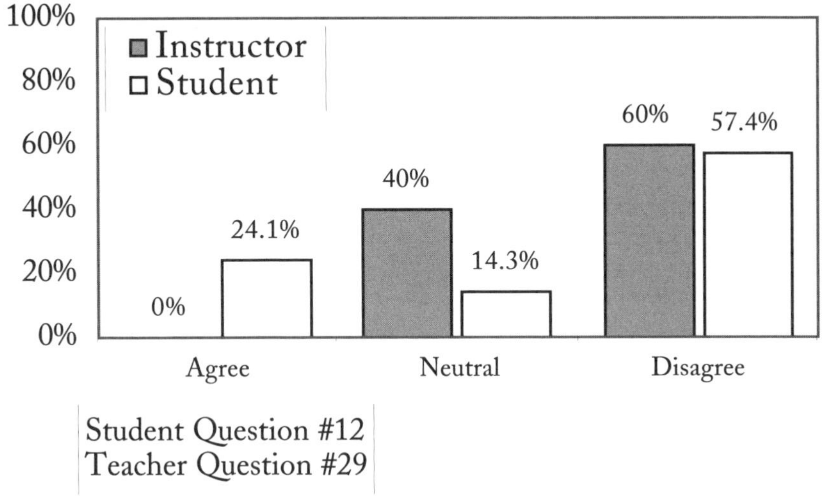

Although the majority in both cases (57% and 60%) saw no similarity, the students' perception echoes claims of researchers who see e-mail as a special form of communication that has features of speaking as well as writing. Apparently students were more conscious of the conversational character of the written discussion than were the instructors.

On the pilot study conducted to assess the comprehensiveness and clarity of the questionnaire, students had been asked what they liked least about the Daedalus software. Seven out of twelve replied that it was the lack of oral practice in their language learning. A question was thus added to the revised questionnaire, to ask students if they preferred computer exchanges to speaking in class. This question sought to distinguish between the perception of speaking (question 12) and the actual preference for speaking or using the InterChange (question 15, whose student questionnaire results are displayed in Figure 5).

FIGURE 5. COMPUTER EXCHANGES VERSUS SPEAKING IN CLASS

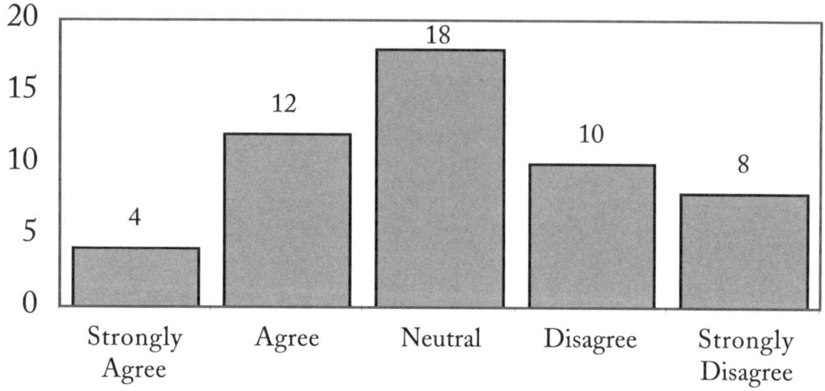

Student Question #15: "I prefer computer exchanges to speaking in class." (N=54)

Interestingly, whereas Figure 4 shows the majority of students do not see a similarity between speaking and InterChange writing, Figure 5 reveals that only slightly more students preferred speaking in class to InterChange communication. The majority were neutral. Taken together, responses to the question of preference seem to be distributed fairly evenly, suggesting that the InterChange excites no striking preferences among participants.

When and How to Use InterChange

Given the current interest in computer-based instruction, knowing how many stations to consider optimal is a key question for administration of computer use fees, as students are well aware. Question 20 thus asked students to consider whether there is an preferable learning stage for using InterChange. They were asked to decide whether its integration in "first-year; second-year; third-year and above, graduate level, or any language course" was most useful for learning/teaching languages. While not a majority, a strong 43% responded that Daedalus InterChange is most useful in "any foreign language course." Secondary preferences were for more advanced undergraduate students (22% preferred second year, 22% third year and above).

With regard to the frequency with which InterChange should be used, of the 79.6% of learners that use InterChange once a week, 20.4% declared that they would like to use it twice a week, although the majority found one weekly session (the actual average for most students) the preferable application. Here again, the distribution of teachers' responses differed from students. Two of the five teachers agreed with the majority of students, that "once weekly" was optimal. Two found "two to three times a semester" preferable. The fifth teacher failed to address the question.

Students were also asked to distinguish between desirable frequency in the abstract and with respect to a specific class, two separate questions. The distribution of student responses suggested they would prefer greater use in general practice than in the specific class in which they were involved (see Figure 6).

FIGURE 6. DESIRED FREQUENCY BASED ON STUDENTS' RESPONSES

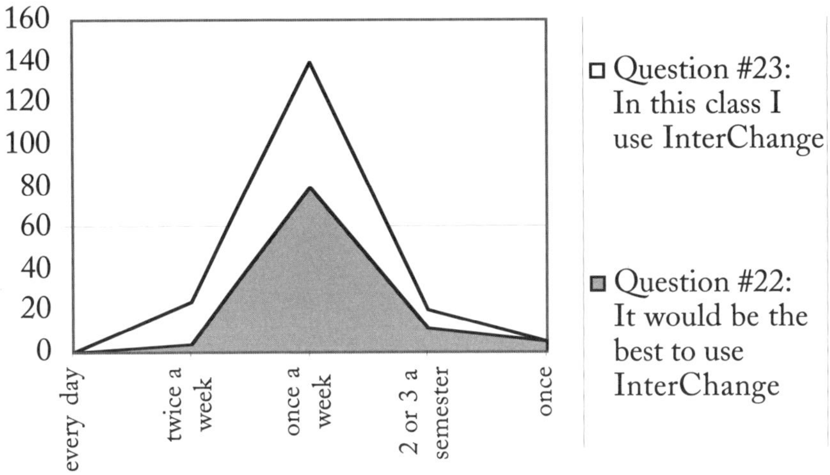

Current versus desired frequency of InterChange use (N=54)

The four out of five teachers who responded to these items answered in less definitive fashion. While two teachers found once weekly appropriate for both their particular class (question 23) and any language class (question 22), the two other respondents selected items that suggested that, in hindsight, they now thought it best use InterChange *less* frequently in their particular class than they would in the abstract (question 22). In retrospect, the framers of the questionnaire would revise the categories so that they would be more sensitive to the instructional setting for foreign language courses at this institution. The courses that use InterChange do so voluntarily and hence for every ten sections of beginning and intermediate

French, German, or Spanish, only three of four each semester avail themselves of this technology. These courses operate, however, with shared syllabi. Realistically, then, by eliminating "every day" and twice weekly, we could then insert "biweekly" and "4 to 5 a semester" as the middle categories which would indicate more precisely actual practice.

Why computer technology is so popular among this sample of FL students remains speculation. However, in their comments (see especially open-ended questions A-D on the questionnaire), students noted most frequently that a change from their everyday routine was beneficial. The second most frequent entry cited curiosity about using new technology as a motivation. In particular, transcripts are cited in the interviews as helpful in giving feedback to students on the screen and also when teachers printed them for distribution and discussion subsequent to InterChange sessions. It should, however, be noted that the computer lab used in these classes has a trained assistant who performs outstanding "trouble shooting" service whenever problems arise. As an appropriate proactive measure for any computer classroom that is to function this well, the presence of a lab assistant is highly recommended.

Contrasting Student and Teacher Views

According to 72.2% of the students, a computer InterChange fits in easily in a foreign language course (see Figure 7), which shows that students do consider perfectly legitimate to use CACD as an effective way of learning foreign language. Teachers, however, were not as sanguine about the ease with which CACD can be incorporated into their course.

In this relatively small sample, teachers attribute their reservations to factors such as syllabus organization, and to difficulties in scheduling hours with the computer laboratory. Several mentioned during oral interviews that they were still experimenting with this new medium and trying to isolate effective techniques, so that they did not feel completely at ease in the lab. Course planning for the computer session was perceived as more challenging than for their usual classes, especially because the freedom given by the CACD could sometimes conflict with a prescriptive or established syllabus (particularly at beginner levels).

An additional concern was with technical problems related to teachers' limited knowledge of how the program worked (login problems, saving documents, locating documents, and the like). In rare instances, for example, students were unable to join the conference right away because of a password or memory problem with the computer. These reservations probably account for the disparity in views between students and teachers, as indicated in Figure 7.

FIGURE 7. EASE OF INTEGRATION

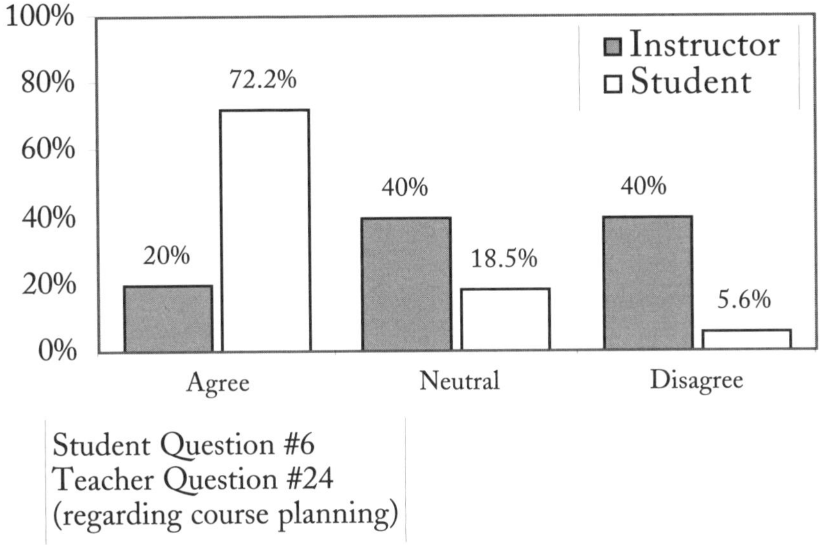

Indeed, teachers' relative unfamiliarity with computers (in contrast to students of a computer generation) may well explain the fact that for 60% (or three of five) instructors polled indicated (as shown in Figure 8),

FIGURE 8. TECHNICAL DIFFICULTIES WITH INTERCHANGE

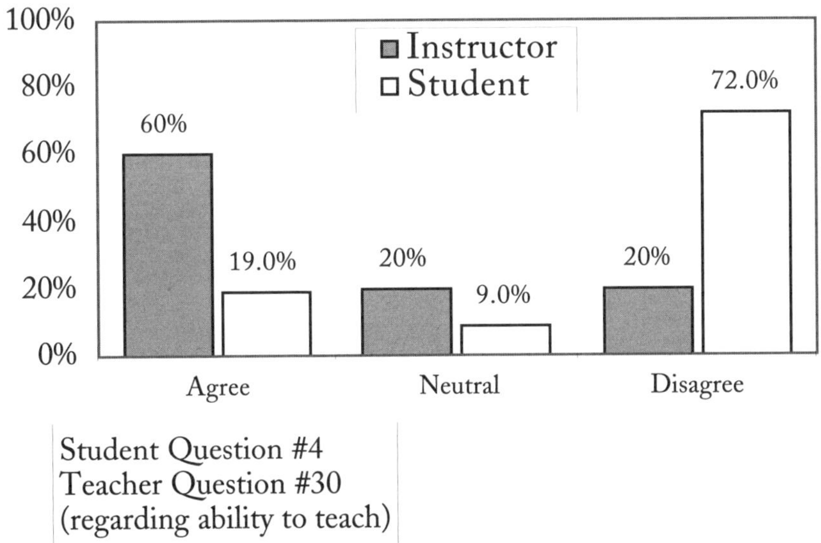

technical difficulties interfered with their use of the Daedalus program. Psychologically, then, teachers reacted with more resistance than did their students when faced with the same technological constraints.

Again, the response in Figure 8 above implies that teachers need more overt technical assistance in handling computers in a pedagogical setting. They want to pay attention to their students, not to the machines their students use. In their interviews, several teachers noted that with this new method they needed to develop new teaching techniques and that preparing a network session demanded as much or more time as preparing a traditional session. However, these same teachers also noted that in CACD very little technical knowledge (as compared, for example, with programming) is necessary. It was with respect to the Daedalus InterChange that four of the five instructors interviewed were positive in response to the question "I feel prepared to teach with computers" (see Appendix A, question 31).

Instructors also stressed that a CACD session was very different from their earlier experiences with the first stages of Computer-Assisted Language Learning. They had earlier identified computer assisted-language programs with mechanistic drill whose goal was enhancing automatic learning. In contrast, they noted that CACD focused on writing of communicatively-meaningful utterances, which were "tested" by the other members of the "writing community" according to their intelligibility and appropriateness.

Conclusion

Results from this questionnaire suggest that foreign language students welcome computer exchanges as a change of pace and find the use of the Daedalus network described here relatively unproblematic. The use of computers and computer networks does not seem to pose concerns for college students today.

Instructors, as might be anticipated, seem to feel more concerned about technical difficulties (Figure 8). Moreover, they tended to prefer fewer computer sessions than did their students. These findings thus suggest that teachers, not students, may be the public to be targeted for assistance in using the computer. Some reluctance on the part of teachers apparently results from unfamiliarity with computer functions and in conjunction with their unease about how to best use the software to maximize learning—the teachers know they know less than their students, in many cases. Interviews with teachers underscored the importance of teacher training, even when software was acknowledged to be extremely user-friendly.

Additional reluctance seems to stem from teachers' concerns about integrating networking into the curriculum (e.g., Figure 7). The fact that, given the hundreds of foreign language sections at this institution, only about ten classes regularly use the computer labs suggests that departments will probably have to hold workshops on integrating this work into specific syllabi before use will become more widespread. One need that research can meet in the future is, thus, to establish whether the perceived benefits attributed to networking in this study are verifiable in actual improvement in writing and / or other skills, when compared to traditional classes. Is networking no more than a "change of pace," or can learner progress be attributed to these exchanges? Further, are some tasks preferable to others? In other words, are there preferable activities or a preferable structure for activities on the network system so that learning is maximized?

From a purely attitudinal standpoint, however, the consonance in viewpoints between students and teachers was consistent with regard to the perceived benefits of networking. Whether considering parallels between reading, listening, or speaking and network activities, misalignment in assessment was rare and a question of degree rather than a massive contrast in opinion. Moreover, the popularity of networking among students and the skill-transfer they identified in their answers were consistent with the findings of the single class survey conducted by Beauvois (1992). In a field where, as suggested by Cohen (1991), all too little consensus exists between students and teachers about "standards" for writing, interactive feedback from peers may well add an intelligibility quotient lacking in teacher corrections of student writing.

References

Barnett, M. A. (1989). Writing as a process. *French Review, 63*, 31-44.

Beauvois, M. H. (1992a). Computer-assisted classroom discussion in the foreign language classroom: Conversation in slow motion. *Foreign Language Annals, 25*, 455-64.

Beauvois, M. H. (1992b). *Computer-assisted classroom discussion in French using networked computers.* Unpublished doctoral dissertation, the University of Texas at Austin.

Bender, R. (1993). ASPECTS: Simultaneous conference software for the Mac. *Calico Journal, 10 (2),* 18.

Brierley, B., & Kemble, I. (1991). *Computers as a tool in language teaching.* New York: Ellis Horwood.

Bump, J. (1990). Radical changes in class discussion using networked computers. *Computers and the Humanities, 24,* 49-65.

Cohen, A. (1991). Feedback on writing. The use of the verbal report. *Studies in Second Language Acquisition, 13,* 133-59.

Dunkel, P. (Ed.). (1990). *Computer-assisted language learning and testing*. New York: Newbury House.

Kelm, O. R. (1992). The use of synchronous computer networks in second language instruction: A preliminary report. *Foreign Language Annals, 25*, 441-54.

Kemp, F. (1993). The Daedalus Integrated Writing Environment. *Educators' Tech Exchange*, Winter, 24-30.

Appendix A

<u>SURVEY</u>: Learning & Teaching Foreign Languages with Computers and Daedalus InterChange

The purpose of this survey is to give you an opportunity to express your opinions about the Daedalus program used in Batts 230 and its InterChange ability(= Classroom Communication through networked computers) for language learning. It takes about 5 minutes to answer this survey: your time and cooperation is highly appreciated!

<u>INSTRUCTIONS</u>:
1. Please, **use a N° 2 pencil** to answer the survey questions on the orange answer sheet. There are 3 pages of questions.
2. **<u>DO NOT FILL IN</u>** the following items on the orange answer sheet, since they will not be used: <u>Last name, first name, grade, Signature, Date, Unique.</u>
3. On the first page of the orange form: **FILL IN** the boxes asking for **your sex, your birth date, and your SSN box (the last four digits are enough); <u>instead of the Instructor</u>, indicate the language you study with Daedalus; <u>instead of the</u> <u>Course</u>, indicate in which semester of language study you are.**
4. Return the completed form to Gary in the Computer Room (Batts 230) or to Christophe Jaeglin, Dept. of Germanic Languages, E.P. Schoch 3.102, 471-8349.

(Please omit any question that doesn't apply)

SCALE:

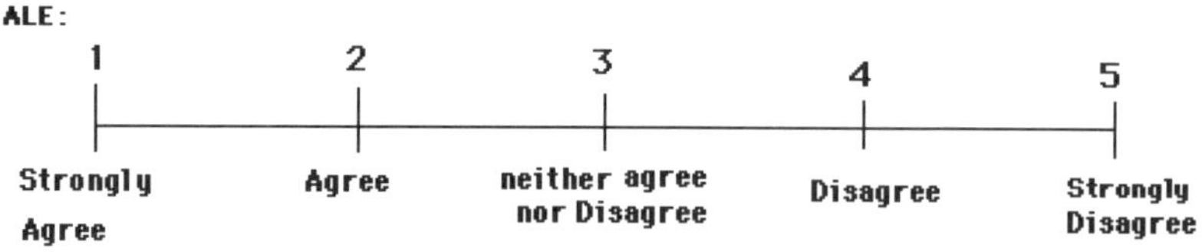

1. My previous experiences with computers have been positive.

2. My experience with computer InterChange in this class is positive.

3. It seems strange to me to communicate using a machine.

4. Mechanical difficulties interfere with my ability to express my thoughts using computers. (e.g. typing skills)

5. The InterChange program used in this class is very easy to use.

6. The InterChange program fits in easily in a language course.

7. I hope other foreign language courses I take will include computer InterChange.

8. As a language learner, I find I learn a great deal when the class engages in small group projects on the computer (2 or 3 students in a private "conference".)

9. When compared with a regular classroom I find a computer InterChange gives me more practice in writing.

10. When compared with a regular classroom I find a computer InterChange gives me more practice in reading.

11. When compared with a listening activity in a regular classroom I find a computer exchange gives me a similar learning opportunity.

12. When compared with a speaking activity in a regular classroom I find a computer exchange gives me a similar learning opportunity.

13. I look forward to a computer InterChange in class.

14. I get anxious before or while using a computer InterChange in class.

15. I prefer computer exchanges to speaking in class.

16. I find conversation on the network chaotic.

17. I find conversations on the network yield interesting discussions.

18. Ideas evolve so quickly on the network that by the time my response is ready, it's already too late to answer.

19. On the computer network answers can be thought through, formulated, and revised carefully before sending to the others.

****

Note: Henceforth the numbers in parenthesis behind the possible answer indicate which of the 5 "bubbles" to fill in on your answer sheet. Answers are NOT related to the scale anymore; For example if the answer to question 20 is "2nd year" you fill out the "bubble" 2 on the answer sheet.

20. The use of the InterChange program is the most useful for learning/teaching languages at university in (pick one): (1) 1st. year (2) 2nd year (3) 3rd year and above (4) graduate level (5) any foreign language course.

21. For me using InterChange on a regular basis means (pick one): (1) every day (2) twice a week (3) once a week (4) once a month (5) two or three times in the semester.

22. I think that it would be the best to use InterChange: (1) every day (2) twice a week (3) once a week (4) two or three times in the semester (5) never.

23. In this class I use the InterChange program: (1) every day (2) twice a week (3) once a week (4) two or three times in the semester (5) once.

LAST FOUR DIGITS OF YOUR ID ____________

This last sheet asks for your comments. PLEASE ANSWER ON THIS SHEET by circling one of the two: 'would' or 'would not' and by adding your comments.

a. I would / would not (circle one) recommend regular use of this InterChange program (Explain why below, citing advantages and/or drawbacks):

---

b. I would / would not (circle one) recommend suggestions for more effective use. Suggested improvements:

---

c. What I like the most in my Daedalus InterChange sessions:

---

d. What I like the least in my Daedalus InterChange sessions:

---

e. OTHER COMMENTS (please indicate "As a student" or "As a teacher")

```
**************************************************
```

<u>This last section ONLY FOR INSTRUCTORS</u>: Please answer on the orange sheet where you left off.

Class(es) taught and level: __________

Language taught: __________

SCALE:

1	2	3	4	5
Strongly Agree	Agree	neither agree nor Disagree	Disagree	Strongly Disagree

24. I find it easy to integrate Daedalus in the planning of my course. (see scale above)

25. I had problems scheduling hours for my course in the computer lab.

26. When compared with a regular classroom I find a computer exchange gives my students more practice in writing.

27. When compared with a regular classroom I find a computer exchange gives my students more practice in reading.

28. When compared with a listening activity in a regular classroom I find a computer exchange gives my students a similar learning opportunity.

29. When compared with a speaking activity in a regular classroom I find a computer exchange gives my students a similar learning opportunity.

30. Technical difficulties interfere with my ability to teach with computers.

31. I feel prepared to teach with computers.

32. In the future I plan to use the computer network (InterChange program) more often with my students.

Notes

[1] The author wishes to thank Marilla D. Svinicki (Center for Teaching Effectiveness, UT Austin) and Elaine Horwitz (Dept. of Education, UT Austin) for their suggestions during initial stages of survey development.

[2] The University Computer Center, Batts 230, is part of the Liberal Arts Media Center at the University of Texas and is designated for sign-up use by foreign language classes on a "first come, first served" basis.

[3] InterChange is the feature of the Daedalus program that allows for synchronous, real-time written communication on the network.

[4] Two transcript formats are available on the current Daedalus InterChange. One presents the actual sequence of statements that appeared during the InterChange session. The other sorts entries by user name, enabling the teacher to return only individual comments to the students.

Section IV

CACD in the Classroom

The two essays in this section, by Kelm and Swaffar, discuss many of the problems and advantages of Computer-Assisted Class Discussion (CACD) in the classroom.

Taking the availability of e-mail as a starting point, Kelm describes how to integrate that kind of asynchronous discussion into the foreign language question. In very pragmatic terms, he discusses access, problems in implementation, grading strategies, and advantages of e-mail message discussions as an alternate way of exposing students to an enhanced L2 environment and to give them more control over the context of language use.

Swaffar talks about issues of assessment and achievement—the practical issues that each teacher must confront when broaching the possibility of actually integrating computers into the curriculum, and what difficulties and decisions individuals might need to make. Her essay offers an assessment measure, conceptual coding, for assessing the kind of progress that seems to characterize students in the CACD classroom. Moreover, she proposes that this measure, based on four levels of discourse complexity, be used to assist students in understanding and measuring their progress.

The Use of Electronic Mail in Foreign Language Classes

Orlando R. Kelm

Introduction

Most researchers and teachers in higher education are aware of the increasingly prominent role that the Internet will play in educational enterprises across disciplines. All text-based networked communication is of great interest to language educators, and whereas the other essays in this volume detail local area network procedures and results, this chapter focuses specifically on distance communication with interlocutors outside the classroom. The wide area communication facilitated by the Internet is particularly significant for L2 language instruction, as it addresses the potential for foreign language students to converse with L1 speakers in their native countries. Currently, formats for teaching using the Internet are multiplying. Electronic mail, or e-mail, is the earliest and simplest.

E-mail is the term for asynchronous message exchange across the Internet world-wide. Early foreign language instruction with computers focused on developing software programs which were electronic versions of traditional workbook assignments. Exercises from the electronic "workbooks" could be assigned as homework, offered as remedial aids, or used for individualized instruction in a computer laboratory. Computer-assisted instruction in open-ended learning situations was even discouraged (Hertz, 1987). However, attitudes towards the use of computers for language learning have changed markedly over the past five years. The effectiveness of computer-based learning is now gauged by improved academic performance, not by the mere presence of a computer in an activity (c.f. Underwood, 1984; Warschauer, 1996a; see also Dunkel, 1991, for an in-depth review of current research on CALL effectiveness).

Moreover, public readiness and ability to implement computer technologies have increased. Computers have become a common part of society's daily activities, and so their use in foreign language instruction may be considered a natural extension of this contact. The technological capacities facilitating distance learning will enhance the various communicative activities that language teachers have come to consider important (Moran, 1992; Warschauer, 1996b). E-mail systems have instructional potential for classroom use similar to that of local area networks because of their most distinctive characteristics: they too allow for one-to-one asynchronous conversations—that is, conversations between a sender and a receiver who do not need to be logged on to a computer at the same time, but who can log on at any time they desire to read or send mail.

What follows describes one possible implementation of e-mail as a tool for foreign-language teaching and communication, given that e-mail accounts are increasingly available to all university students. Such an implementation is the natural consequence of advances in technology, but it represents a case where the technology has advanced faster than its applications in our classrooms. Although teachers use e-mail regularly for their personal and professional communication, implementing this technology as a learning aid is a phenomenon only under development at best. Current technology is poised for classroom implementations.

Class Profile

In response to this situation, an approach to Portuguese e-mail correspondence as a learning activity was introduced for students in their fourth semester of language training at the University of Texas at Austin.[1] In the particular e-mail experiment reported here, twelve students participated: six undergraduates (two of whom were native speakers of Spanish), and six graduate students (three of whom were native speakers of Spanish). Of the twelve, only one had not studied Spanish previously, and that student had spent some time in Portugal. These students attended class three days a week for two hours each class, over a period of fifteen weeks.

As part of course requirements, students were required to write at least 50 lines of e-mail messages in Portuguese every week. They were free to communicate with anyone about any topic, as long as the messages were in Portuguese, since our main concern was communication, not practice in any particular topic or discourse style. The students sent a copy of each message to me as course instructor, which I used to offer error corrections and to grade. Students knew that they could particularly expect comments on spelling errors, grammar, and (crucial for this group) Spanish transfers. However, they also knew that their grade was based on completing a minimum of 50 lines a week, and not on grammar *per se*.

Students also had the option of writing their messages to three general groups: 1) students of Portuguese at other American universities,[2] 2) various Brazilians living all over the world, and 3) other students in their class.

The sections which follow describe these students' experience with such e-mail assignments, first in terms of implementation (how students actually started off on an e-mail system), and then in terms of their classroom applications.

Implementing E-Mail Communications for Students

The success of an e-mail program stands and falls on a clear set of practical issues that are usually resolvable on a college or university campus, but which need to be addressed as part of planning for the course.

The physical set-up of e-mail for students in foreign language classes at post-secondary institutions is not complicated.[3] It is appropriate to mention at this point that neither students nor their faculty need to be computer geniuses to take advantage of computer technology. It is helpful to think of computers in the same way people think about cars. Nobody expects the average driver to know all the intricate details of how car engines operate before driving to work. Car owners buy whatever car is most appropriate to their desires and budget. Similarly, users do not have to understand technical aspects of mainframe computing before they log on to an existing e-mail system for personal use.

With this practical metaphor in mind, what follows are some suggestions and procedures for the implementation of e-mail activities for university and college students. While specific applications for the foreign-language class will be addressed later, the suggestions made here refer to most college and university instructional contexts, and they can be used for situations where students will be expected to complete any type of assignment outside of class, using their access to an e-mail system at their own convenience.

1. Obtaining Computer Accounts for Access to a Mainframe Computer

The first step in initiating electronic mail service for students is to provide them a way to gain access to a mainframe computer—to a large centralized computer that is connected to the Internet. A recent survey reports that 84% of university students and/or faculty members have access to such mainframe computers (Hirschheim, Smithson, & Whitehouse, 1990, p. 63).

Students generally open their accounts and receive user ID numbers from a university computing center. Depending on the available computer systems, the mainframe computer they will access will be one of numerous acronyms, such as IBM, UNIX, VAX, SUN, and others. Fortunately, for the purpose of e-mail access, it does not matter which mainframe students use—they just need to ascertain that their mainframe is networked with other mainframes through the country and world.

For example, most students at the University of Texas at Austin use UNIX systems since they are available to them very economically. Students pay only a nominal fee each semester to open and maintain their computer privileges here. Some institutions charge students nothing at all; others require teachers to request computer time and funds before the start of each class or each academic year and specify dedicated time to particular classes for instructional purposes only. Still others may or may not charge for network access or for messages, but may require cash deposits to cover printing and CPU time. Regardless of expense to the user or other conditions, though, all such available systems have the capability of connecting students to Internet.

2. *Getting Started: Logon and Logoff Procedures*

Students who have never used the computer before will need help in logging on and off for the first time, establishing passwords for their accounts, and learning some basic keystrokes. They also need to be taught how to address messages (e.g., fulano@mail.utexas.edu).

The best way to do this is to sit down individually with students and walk them through the steps as they log on for the first time. We use the freeware version of "Eudora" for both the Macintosh and IBM. Eudora serves as an interface which connects the user to his/her mail account via a modem or internet-style network connection. The situation at the University of Texas is typical: depending on which computer lab students choose to use, the terminals available are different and require a slightly different set of keystrokes to do the same things.

If your students only use one type of terminal, they will have an easier time learning. If, however, the possibility exists for them to work from many different types of terminals, they will need help in learning the equivalencies between terminal types and a parallel set of log on instructions for each terminal. Note, too, that this training does not always have to come from the teacher of a particular class: if a mainframe exists, help and documentation are *always* available from university or college computation centers, and training sessions are usually provided regularly throughout the school year.

3. *Other Training and Practice Sessions on the Computer*

For the average class of students who will be using e-mail, it is generally worthwhile to spend at least one initial class period in a computer lab together. During this time, students should learn and practice basic commands for writing and sending messages. Most computer centers provide appropriate handouts with log on and log off examples, as well as a list of frequent commands that will be useful during such training classes (and beyond).

Students will also learn at this time that access to mainframe computers always requires the use of a personal password. It is important to emphasize the security of such passwords. Students who use their first names as passwords, may be rudely surprised. Computer hackers can enter their account files, steal their money (their "paid" computer time or print-out funds), and then close their accounts. A truly secure password necessitates, however, that students keep a personal record of that password on their person. Security cuts both ways and students tend to forget their passwords or details about them such as abbreviations or lower case entries. A readily available record to check against will help forestall the need to create a new "secret" password.

Most students only need one initial training session. However, others may need a little extra help to get over their fear of using computers. Additionally, it is not uncommon for students to try and help each other to become more acquainted with computer usage. For example, the following message was sent by a class member after receiving help from a classmate[4]:

Oi M, obrigado pela ajuda que você mandou. Estou obrigado também por ensinar a mim os computadores de Taylor. São mais bons e mais fáceis do que os outros.

Hi, M, thanks for the help that you sent. I am also thankful for your teaching me about the computers in Taylor [Hall, a computer center]. They are better and easier than the others.

The students work well together via computer in this way. In the situation described here, they not only provided help about computer problems, but they also prepared and sent each other language exercises and clarified questions related to grammar or assignments.

Classroom Applications

For the use of e-mail to be a success in any particular class, the teacher must be able to integrate the student's use of e-mail messages into classroom activities and assessment of performance. Students dedicate a lot of time to reading, writing, and sending messages. It is thus only fair that grading procedures and course activities reflect a proper balance and evaluation of the time and emphasis given to the project.

What follow are some suggestions for reaching such a balance in the average foreign language classroom. Each is based on experience with students of Portuguese at the University of Texas, and so may need modification for other situations or for other types of students.

1. Writing Requirements and Grading

As already noted, students send a copy of all their correspondence to the course instructor. This is done for two reasons. First, the copy documents whether each student is writing the required number of lines. Second, it helps the instructor provide correction for language errors. Moreover, both uses of correspondence copies help instructors in assigning grades, an unavoidable part of any academic teaching situation, even in a language course whose objective is to promote "natural" target language communication.

Assignments are structured around the number of e-mail lines a student sends a week. As noted, the Portuguese program reported on here requires 50 lines a week, but this assignment length is set for a class that also completes many other writing exercises during the typical semester (including a weekly journal that is screened for grammar content, and in-class writing discussions on a synchronous computer network with InterChange software; see Kelm, 1992). The 50-line requirement, balanced with these additional writing activities, is still well within the capacities of every student.

For grading purposes, then, the student earns a designated number of credit points for each 50-line week, and a percentage of that score if s/he writes fewer than 50. This system is most sensible if late work is not accepted—a requirement that reflects the on-going nature of computer discussion. It is thus not possible for a student to try to write 750 lines in the last week of a semester as part of a last-minute effort to salvage a grade.

2. Grammar Correction

When it comes to grammar review, by the time students get to the fourth semester of language instruction, they generally feel that they have heard it all before. The written transcripts of e-mail messages that a student receives overcome this situation to a degree, since they are confronted with their own language errors and with evidence about how those errors affect communication.

While pedagogical techniques that help students correct these writing and grammar errors are too numerous to review here, three methods that capitalize on the e-mail environment are suggested in this essay.

1) Individualized Grammar Exercises

Each student receives a hard copy of his or her messages, on which grammar and vocabulary mistakes are highlighted (not corrected). The students are assigned the task of correcting the highlighted mistakes and returning the hard copies with the homework.

2) E-Mail Grammar Corrections

The instructor of this course should also participate in the e-mail discussion, preferably with at least one e-mail message to each student once a week. Along with topical comments, these messages give teachers the opportunity to make suggestions and corrections based on the non-standard linguistic features he or she has observed in students' messages to their regular correspondents. The students recognize that this instructional communication is an important part of the program. In fact, the following example shows a student acknowledging that this feedback is an essential feature:

Eu estou bem, mas sinto um pouco triste porque Orlando [instructor] me reprimenda por ter gramatica defeituoso. Bom, gosto de escrever cartas, mas nao gosto de ter cuidado com a gramatica. E bom que ele me reprimenda!!	I'm doing fine, but I feel a little sad because Orlando reprimanded me for my defective grammar. Well, I like to write letters, but I don't like to have to worry about grammar. It is good that he reprimands me!!

For a language instructor, one of the most difficult aspects of teaching is knowing when to step in and provide formal correction. Correct grammar cannot dominate to the point where communication is not allowed to take place. At the same time, correct form does not need to be eliminated from language teaching in order to preserve "communicative competence." By writing e-mail messages to the students, instructors are able to fine-tune grammar errors which affected communication. Yet since the communication has already taken place (successfully or not), the instructor is merely providing personal (not public and potentially embarrassing) suggestions for improving future e-mail communication.

3) In-Class Grammar Exercises

Instructors may also use the e-mail transcripts to prepare grammar exercises and review sessions for the whole class based on mistakes common to many students. Consequently, classroom grammar exercises are based on student sentences—on students' communicative needs and abilities.

For example, since Spanish-fluent students of Portuguese frequently transfer Spanish demonstrative pronouns—esto, estos—to Portuguese, for one week's assignment an instructor can search files and copy all the cases where students use the wrong demonstrative pronouns. Similarly, for another week's assignment, the teacher can create a list of all student sentences in the indicative that require the subjunctive or review all student sentences containing incorrect prepositions. By helping students identify problems in their own language use rather than in textbook models, teachers focus on self-correction as a premise of the student learning.

Analysis, I: A Focus on Real Communication

One of the major objectives in implementing e-mail message writing is to provide students with an increased opportunity to communicate in the target language. As Rivers (1987, p. 3) amplifies, "[S]tudents achieve facility in *using* a language when their attention is focused on conveying and receiving authentic messages (that is, messages that contain information of interest to speaker and listener in a situation of importance to both)." The e-mail environment fills this bill exactly.

Since the students enjoy writing to friends, the emphasis in e-mail message writing almost automatically shifts from "writing in Portuguese" to "writing to friends." In many ways, this process sets up a scenario with goals similar to those of content-based foreign language instruction (e.g., Brinton, Snow, & Wesche, 1990). One student's statement illustrates this contention: she mentioned that she felt her Portuguese had improved during the semester because "I actually wrote letters that people understood and within the next week I got responses and corrections." It clearly is motivating to realize that people really can communicate ideas in this new language. Another student expressed similar sentiments when he wrote the following comments to a classmate:

Estou muito feliz nesta aula porque estamos fazendo coisas especiasis como usando estos computadores loucos por exemplo. Tambem gosto de que podemos practicar tendo conversas.	I am very happy in this class because we are doing special things like using these crazy computers for example. I also like it that we can practice having conversations.

Although the communication with another writer is real in one sense, it should be borne in mind that the students are also aware of the fact that the instructor is "listening" to the conversations. For example, at times the students wrote asides to the instructor during their communications to others:

Eu gosto muito da aula de Orlando (d'ya catch that plug Orlando?)	I really like Orlando's class (d'ya catch that plug Orlando?)

However, on another occasion the same student who wrote this comment was surprised to find out that his instructor knew that he collected old comic books. Although informed at the outset of class and on the syllabus that exchanges would be read by the teacher, the real communication rather than pedagogical practices were foremost in this student's mind. It had not occurred to him that the teacher was monitoring e-mail messages written to another student. In this sense, then, the e-mail assignments are "real communications."

Analysis, II: Student Observations and Opinions

A language-learning activity can be considered successful when students want to continue it after the semester is over, and this response certainly applies to e-mail. Several students wrote to me saying that they wanted to keep their accounts open to continue communication with Brazilians and to practice their Portuguese. In fact, two of the students in Portuguese plan on enrolling in Accelerated Italian next semester. They each have a few friends who will also be in that class, and they all want to practice Italian with each other via e-mail message writing, continuing voluntarily the classroom practices described here.

Several students wrote messages to me at the end of the semester to share their feelings on the value of using e-mail as part of the course. They stressed the value of a communication mode that allowed them "time to think." The students also recognized the value of communicating with Brazilians. One member of the class mentioned that "exposure to Brazilians was a good way to see how Portuguese is actually used." Additionally, students recognized that e-mail message writing increased their use of the target language outside of class.

Such positive feedback is familiar to researchers of classroom uses for computers, but they are strong confirmations of the advantages of e-mail when they come from students and are largely unsolicited.

E-Mail Disadvantages

Although advantages of using e-mail message writing for language practice seem to outweigh disadvantages, several challenges will be posed for instructors implementing these assignments.

First, especially for the students who have had little experience on the computer, initial attempts can be frustrating. The actual difficulties rarely match a student's fears and anxieties, but it is important to reassure those who are apprehensive that their grade in Portuguese is not contingent upon their expertise with a computer.

An early comment by one student in the class described here illustrates the initial fear that accompanies first-time users:

Sim, gosto de barulhos na computadora porque devo fazer algo com uma certa mexcla de alegria de fazer chegar minha mensagem e raiva da posibilidade de que minha mensagem nunca chegue.	Yes, I like the noises of the computer because it creates a certain mixture of joy that my message will get there and anger at the possibility that my message will never arrive.

Significantly, even these mixed feelings were communicated in Portuguese. In a traditional classroom setting, such asides or comments are almost always communicated in English.

Mechanical difficulties have other faces, as well. Since the students may at first be limited in their computer or typing abilities, they may send messages that they would have preferred to change. For example, one student initially didn't know how to edit her comments. As a result, she sent messages that she would have preferred to correct:

As mulheres pensam mais nos sentimentos das pessoas. Bom, sei que isto é sexista, mas não posso borrar o que escrevi porque não sei como usar o "edit mode."	Women think more about people's feelings. Well, I know that is sexist, but I can't erase what I wrote because I don't know how to use the "edit mode."

This student could have edited her passage but apparently had not learned or forgotten that feature of her communications software. Because desire to communicate is inhibited if students feel uncomfortable about any aspect of the exchange (whether real or imagined), it is important for instructors to verify that all students feel comfortable about using the computers.

The other disadvantage of e-mail is specific to second-language learners. Most editing software makes it difficult for students to use accent marks and other foreign diacritics. Although this problem will gradually disappear as programmers meet user demands, in the meantime it seems reasonable to recall that native speakers of Portuguese use e-mail without worrying about the absence of accent marks. These native speakers of Portuguese use this form of communication to share ideas—and apparently without worrying about diacritics. Moreover, as long as grammar follow-up is part of the course, no serious fossilization problems should result for students who type messages without all of the accent marks.

Conclusions: Implications for Future Research

In a foreign language program that wants to increase the amount of real second-language communication that takes place among students, e-mail message writing has provided my class with a medium to exchange ideas in the target language (see also Esling, 1991; Lunde, 1990). Like Morgan and Trainor (1990, p. 64), I have found that in the process of using computer conversations student work has become less passive, more participatory, and more imaginative. Consequently, considering the positive aspects of my experience with Portuguese e-mail conversations, the increased use of the target language by students, and the optimistic feedback from student participants, I am anxious to introduce synchronic messaging (using Daedalus InterChange) in the Portuguese language classroom, as well. Alternately, I would recommend e-mail messaging for classes on campuses with this technical capacity but no local area network capabilities.

Notwithstanding my enthusiasm, it is important to emphasize that no direct claims are being made here about cause-and-effect relationships between e-mail message writing and speaking proficiency. Students probably will still need ample opportunities to express themselves orally in the target language. However, the latest version (3.1) of Eudora includes "PureVoice" which allows for audio attachments that do not use up very much memory. We now have a way of sending audio back and forth via e-mail.

Finally, the anecdotal experience described here suggests a need for empirical examination of what students actually learn in e-mail settings. I thus agree with Dunkel (1991, p. 20), who proposes the need for more non-technocentric research about language learning with computers. "Technocentric" research focuses on the traditional comparison of a control group (without computers) to a treatment group (with computers). The non-technocentric research I am suggesting would allow us to focus, for example, on which L2 skill(s) students acquire while implementing e-mail, which level a proficiency a student should have if s/he is to benefit most from the experience, or how involved teachers should be in e-mail exchanges.

References

Brinton, D. M., Snow, M. A., & Wesche, M. B. (1990). *Content-based second language instruction*. New York: Newbury House.

Chun, D. M., & Brandl, K. K. (1992). Beyond form-based drill and practice: Meaning-enhancing CALL on the Macintosh. *Foreign Language Annals, 25*(3), 255-67.

Cooper, M.M., and Selfe, C. L. (1990). Computer conferences and learning: Authority, resistance, and internally persuasive discourse. *College English, 52* (8), 847-69.

Dunkel, P. (1991). Research on the effectiveness of computer-assisted instruction and computer-assisted language learning. In Dunkel, P. (Ed.), *Computer-assisted Language learning and testing: Research issues and practice* (pp. 5-36). New York: Newbury House.

Esling, J. H. (1991). Researching the effects of networking: Evaluating the spoken and written discourse generated by working with CALL. In Dunkel, P. (Ed.), *Computer-assisted language learning and testing: Research issues and practice* (pp. 111-131). New York: Newbury House.

Hertz, R. M. (1987). *Computers in the language classroom*. Menlo Park, CA: Addison-Wesley.

Hirschheim, R., Smithson, S., & Whitehouse, D. (1990). *Microcomputers and the humanities: Survey and recommendations*. New York: Ellis Horwood.

Holdstein, D. H., & Selfe, C. L. (Eds.) (1990). *Computers and writing: Theory, research, practice*. New York: Modern Language Association.

Kelm, O. R. (1992). The use of synchronous computer networks in second language instruction: A preliminary report. *Foreign Language Annals, 25 (5)*, 441-454.

Lunde, K.R. (1990). Using electronic mail as a medium for foreign language study and instruction. *CALICO Journal, 7 (3)*, 68-78.

Moran, C. (1992). Computers and English: What do we make of each other? *College English, 54 (2)*, 193-98.

Morgan, N. J., & Trainor, R. H. (1990). Liberator or libertine?: The computer in the history classroom. In D. S. Miall (Ed.), *Humanities and the Computer* (pp. 61-70). Oxford: Clarendon Press.

Rivers, W. M. (Ed.) (1987). *Interactive language teaching*. Cambridge: Cambridge University Press.

Underwood, J. H. (1984). *Linguistics, computers, and the language teacher*. Rowley, MA: Newbury House.

Warschauer, M. (1996a). *Computer-mediated collaborative learning: Theory and practice* (Research Note #17). Honolulu: University of Hawai'i, Second Language Teaching & Curriculum Center.

Warschauer, M. (1996b). Motivational aspects of using computers for writing and communication. In M. Warschauer (Ed.), *Telecommunication in foreign language learning: Proceedings of the Hawaii symposium* (pp. 29-46). Honolulu: University of Hawai'i, Second Language Teaching & Curriculum Center.

Notes

[1]It is worth noting that this program capitalizes on our unique situation regarding Portuguese. We can be reasonably sure that our students will be fluent in (or at least familiar with) Spanish before they begin Portuguese. Due to the similarities between these two languages, the students are able to communicate in Portuguese from the initial stages of their language training on. Moreover, nearly all the students in our program are highly motivated to learn the language for personal or professional reasons. To be realistic, not many students learn Brazilian Portuguese simply to complete a language requirement.

[2]I would especially like to thank Professor Antonio Simões of the University of Kansas (Lawrence), whose students actively exchange e-mail with ours.

[3][Editor's Note:] Because of equipment limitations, the situation at secondary schools for such programs is considerably different. For information on a very successful implementation of a variant on an e-mail program at a magnet school with limited computer access, contact Mary Farquhar at Lowell High School, 1101 Eucalyptus Dr., San Francisco, CA 94132.

[4]All the Portuguese examples have been reproduced without editing the student's comments. The translations, however, are provided in standard English.

Assessing Development in Writing: A Proposal for Strategy Coding

Janet Swaffar

As the earlier chapters in this volume document, the Computer-Assisted Classroom Discussion (CACD) in a networked classroom (on a local area network—LAN—or on e-mail) forms a distinctive environment for teaching and learning. Students seem to enjoy the control they have over the environment, are willing to write more to each other than they conventionally do to their teacher, and learn discourse-management tactics that should improve their writing—tactics such as elaboration, modification, and self-correction that foster the typical students' sense that writing is a process that leads to successful communication.

Yet many questions remain about the kind of learning that happens in a networking environment, especially about the relationship between the "speech" or "discussions" on a network and whether they affect the processes that result in excellence in formal writing. These issues are faced by both first and second-language classes. In the case of the second-language classes discussed in this volume, do the behaviors that virtually all the studies above confirm lead to writing that can be more readily understood and responded to that writing practiced in more traditional ways? If that issue can be addressed, then teachers can set about deciding whether networking in any language setting can further traditional essay-writing goals—the writing outcomes appropriate for the academic community at large.

Considering it as a potential tool with which to address these questions, this chapter explores an evaluative measure—a weighting system—that assigns different point values to clauses according to whether or not they reveal strategic discourse management. The measure strives to foreground students' cognitive activity expressed in connected discourse written on a network. That is, it suggests a way of assessing the level of thinking students use when writing. Thus, this coding does not focus on mechanics or purely linguistic features of language use. Instead, teachers identify and assess different values to four different speech acts realized as rhetorical types: 1) descriptive sentences, 2) sentences that express opinions, 3) sentences that have logical features to substantiate opinion, and 4) sentences that establish a logical argument for a point of view. The assigned value of a clause depends on how it communicates these distinctions in the written text as a whole. Normative accuracy, then, in the sense of grammatical or authoritative accuracy in word usage and individual sentences is not the basis for assessing values. Instead, focus is on contextual clarity, the speech act or rhetorical gesture made by a clause in its integrative function within a paragraph or essay.

To illustrate how to weight or attribute different values to clauses, two writing samples, one sample written in the second and one in the last week of a fifth semester college course in German composition will be coded.[1] In the case discussed here, strategy coding seemed appropriate for analyzing and evaluating the work of a sample class in which one third of actual seat time was spent in networking, a task whose objective is to foster the exchange of ideas. The aim here is to illustrate this system for primary trait scoring, i.e., as it assigns a holistic score to a particular feature of writing (Perkins, 1983), and to demonstrate its potential as a diagnostic and research tool that registers strategy development: a writer's ability to argue cogently and exhibit rhetorical, not just grammatical, control of a speech act.[2]

This discussion, therefore, suggests that strategy coding may provide a measure of student improvement that can supplement measures that focus on normative organization and / or linguistic correctness. To put the case another way, this essay looks at writing as a series of connected speech acts that are situationally regulated. To illustrate, students debating the pros and cons of the Republican's Contract with America will probably not use the same language or style as those writing about what they plan to do during Spring vacation. Discussions about the Republican Congress will more likely result in statements reflecting points of view to be defended or argued. Vacation plans will more likely elicit speech acts intended only to inform, rhetorical gestures adequately expressed in speech acts characterized by descriptive clauses ("I'm spending my vacation in the library"). To communicate a point of view involves a cognitive synthesis or strategic control of one's own position and features of the issue debated ("I've got so many papers to write that I'm spending my vacation in the library"). Moreover, writers must both know what they want to say and then be able to signal that intent to others.

Nonetheless, students writing about the most innocuous topics display different degrees of strategic control. For example, the student who explains *why* she is spending her vacation in the library has not only provided more information to the reader, she has also established the rationale motivating her decision. Fellow students know on what grounds to applaud or question the wisdom of her choice ("I tried that last year and didn't get anything accomplished"). Sentences that tell "why" an opinion is given or a particular course of action taken are, thus, not only more informative, they also provide the basis for exchanging ideas. As syntheses of two concepts (the "what" and the "why" of a statement), they inevitably reveal more complex morphosyntax than simple descriptions or opinions in and of themselves.

Teachers who pose controversial topics for discussion are more likely to see examples of strategic management because the difference between a substantiated and unsubstantiated opinion reveals a writer's strategic control of her rhetorical gesture. The statement sequence "How can Republicans claim to have a contract on the basis of an election? Contracts aren't elected." in the context of a discussion about the Contract with American presents a speaker intent (arguing against the validity of the concept "contract" as used by the Republicans) and the basis for that argument (the definition of a contract). Fellow students may react in high dudgeon or jump in to agree, but either way, the writer has successfully communicated an intent to criticize and a basis for criticism by calling the term "contract" into question (it is "one-way").

Whether responses are vehement or supportive, the writer has engaged in a successful speech act, not a misfire (Searle, 1969). Had the student written "Contractual agreements are generally binding between two parties," he would have produced a simple description of fact, which, in spite of its elegant English, would fail to do more than provide one definition of contract. The intent of the description would, without further elaboration, remain unclear. Even, the assertion "I hate contracts," although it signals an intent, does not establish a basis on which to agree, disagree, or ask the person to elaborate ("Why do you hate contracts?"). The scope of this particular communication is limited, because the rhetorical strategy reflects only opinion without the basis for that opinion. However, if the descriptive sentence followed the assertion ("I hate contracts. Contractual agreements are generally binding between two parties."), the reader could at least infer a writer intent—that of not wishing to be bound or tied down.

When teachers perceive a discoverable relationship between what students intend to write and how readers of that message respond, they can say with some certainty that students are able to manage their discourse, providing readers with sufficient information to understand what speech act they intend to communicate and why. The objective of the coding suggested here is to enable both teachers and students to monitor success in this style of strategic situation management. When student writing in computer classrooms reveals increasing control in persuading, arguing, or explicating writer views, then teachers can say with some assurance that time spent on computer networking is time well spent.

The Case for a New Measure for Effective Written Communication

In the past twenty years, communicative emphases in ESL and FL classrooms have moved from a focus on form to a focus on the exchange of ideas. Yet our measures for assessing written performance of students who learn in these communicative situations are largely limited to formal features or holistic grading systems. From a different perspective, research in L2 writing lacks follow-up studies to see whether student writing continues to reveal improvement under constraints different from those in which they learned (e.g. Santos, 1989; Kroll, 1990). Does, for instance, the ability to negotiate a situation in the real world linguistically correlate with other forms of production, such as essay writing? Clearly, then, this and many other questions remain at issue for the teacher or researcher seeking to assess student achievement (e.g., Carrell, & Connor, 1991).

A second set of questions about student achievement remain from the students' point of view, as well. In a classroom, for example, how does assessment feed into further learning? What kind of diagnosis is most beneficial for students being assessed? Fathman and Whalley's findings (1990) argue for correction that addresses both message and form, for example. While Kepner (1991) found that formal correction in isolation yielded negligible effects, she did not include the combination of form/ message correction in her research design—a type of correction that would seem to value success or failure within a communication situation, not just formal accuracy in a more purely linguistic sense.

If one turns from more general studies about student achievement to research in L2 writing, research clarifying what and how students actually learn is even scarcer than on error correction or communicative competence: the corpus of research in L2 writing is relatively small, and virtually no replication studies exist. The larger corpus of research on second-language learning in general suggests that students seem to learn forms when they are ready, not necessarily when they are taught. At the same time, increased grammaticality in language use seems to result from complex combinations of learned skills, involving not only bottom-up processing skills, but also learned patterns of negotiation in meaning, social function, and discourse structure (Celce-Murcia, 1991, p. 478). Since the learning that must take place if students are to progress to advanced levels is so complex, it is no wonder that most longitudinal studies reveal negligible effects on syntactical improvement of spontaneous speech following instruction in, for example, the copula in equational sentences, negation, or WH questions (e.g., Larsen-Freeman, & Long, 1991, 304-9).

By analogy, then, the kind of data used in the studies above—documenting one class session's to one semester's work on improving structural features in written composition—is unlikely to document dramatic differences in morphosyntactic use between early and late writing samples, no matter how much more writing students produce or how much more students prefer the medium or environment in which that writing is produced. The samples scored in this paper are no exception to that general principle.

As in L1 essay evaluation, then, questions arise about whether competence in writing should be assessed only or primarily for composing that reflects strategic control of intent (negotiating meanings, managing situations) rather than as a specific linguistic competence, usually defined as morphosyntactic competence (Kroll, 1990, p. 49). Consequently, the practice used in assessing writing on many standardized writing placement examinations (and increasingly in research studies as well) tries to combine holistic measures that rate rhetorical features such as cohesion, coherence, content, and organization in conjunction with formal linguistic features, grouping them under categories such as mechanics (morphology and punctuation), syntax, and vocabulary (e.g., Brown, 1991).

In order to analyze these issues from other perspectives, other research tools for assessing compositional strategies have been developed, to look at sentence types in the writing produced, or to characterize the sentence unit itself (the T-unit) in a way that can assess whether student writing exhibits increased control of discursive situations. While the ability to write at length is generally acknowledged as one measure of a student's growing facility in a foreign language, teachers are all too familiar with the fact that such increased quantity can also reflect a student's growing verbosity or empty formulaic speech rather than a facility to convey substantive messages in more sophisticated ways. Hence these measures of quantity are again frequently augmented with holistic assessments of content and organization (e.g., Kern, 1992). While such measures offer clear views to new kinds of research on student achievement, they rarely seem applicable to the classroom in the way that assessments of syntax or rhetorical organization do: holistic assessments rarely reveal to the writer ways to change sentence units so that they present content more convincingly or develop clearer organizational links between ideas.

One popular research tool developed to assess the number of ideas a student uses in written or spoken discourse is the idea unit. As usually defined, idea units are the number of concepts *within* sentences. As such, they look at constituent components of clauses, to offer a picture of the relationship between the number and quality of words and syntactical forms used, and the number of ideas actually contained in that quantity of words—ideas whose place in a coherent system of grammatically correct thought is often difficult to measure. Idea units are, moreover, not necessarily a positive feature as regards clarity (as teachers know all too well).

Thus, for example, a writer compressing many ideas into one sentence may well cloud, rather than clarify, her intent, requiring a high level of interpretation by a listener, reader, or researcher to ascertain whether too much is being said, or essentially an inarticulate nothing. This aspect of working with idea units renders them difficult to use as a research tool, although teachers often offer their students prompts for improving their writing in just these terms ("what's the central idea here?" or "your idea is unclear"). One additional problem accompanies the use of idea units as an assessment measure. Because they assess pieces of a whole discourse rather than connected whole thought (topics and comments), idea units on the sentence level cannot be coded for their discursive relationships, only for conceptual ones—that is, the researcher is not able to behave like a teacher and untangle what a student meant in an earlier sentence by recourse to a later one (by using discourse-level interpretive strategies rather than sentence-level ones).

Another measure used in research assesses coherence and cohesion in writing. Traditionally, discourse analysis measures cohesive ties within bodies of produced language or essays by looking at intersentential connections of semantic features such as pronominal reference and substitutions (e.g., "That's a wonderful day *dog*. I want *one*."). As indices about how language relates ideas, such measures yield insights into the ways to use syntactic and semantic features of a language to clarify meaning and "manage" the hearer's or reader's understanding of language produced. Because of their attention to connections within a discourse, however, these discourse analysis measures do not usually yield insights into the logical cogency of the propositional *concepts* that are being related. Discourse analysis too often addresses surface forms of language in context in terms of competence, not necessarily the appropriateness of content/concept links. Again, then, a teacher of essay writing may object that certain paragraphs are beautifully written (i.e., are coherent and cohesive and correct)—but they "do not say much" or could be radically reduced and still say the same thing. Competent discourse does not always signal that writer's ability to engage in strategic situation management, avoiding misfires and expressing his or her intent in a fashion intelligible to others.

From a psycholinguistic perspective, all of the foregoing measures have limitations for any program that tries to use these tools for assessment to outline to students what clear writing that presents substantive ideas might be. Holistic or metalinguistic measures tend to be too global to link to classroom practice or suggest specific modes for improvement. On the other hand, formal correction or accuracy coding pinpoints problems but may be insensitive to other variables that affect accuracy such as task and the cohesiveness of the discourse—the point of the utterance, not just its form (Parrish, & Tarone, 1986), for example.

More importantly, formal correction will probably fail to diagnose progress made within a single semester, since interlanguage studies suggest a much longer period is needed before input registers as output in this way—the student will notice not only, for example, that their computer transcript from late in a semester is longer and tries to say more, but also how many errors still remain. Teachers may, in such a case, be hard-pressed to make clear that a student may progress linguistically in ways other than morphosyntactic accuracy. Finally, for those teacher / assessors interested in specifying the content of a written essay, these methods may be able to quantify idea units in an essay, but they fail to measure whether and how purposefully a longer statement's ideas connect, as discourse or task fulfillment, to meet a student's objection that "it's long enough, and every sentence and paragraph is largely correct and makes sense."

Small wonder, then, that "the largest and best known assessment programs manage to achieve a reader reliability score of between .70 to .80 level" (Santos, 1989, p. 712)—or that teachers who are asked to grade against any of these more holistic standards are not able to grade essays and come up with equivalent grades more than 80% of the time, in contrast to expectations about grammatical correction. While statistically significant, this variance points out that various scoring measures have large grey areas about what they actually assess—areas subject to considerable interpretation. Neither holistic grading for cohesion, content, and organization on the one hand, nor discrete grading based on discourse analysis, T-units, idea units, mechanics, syntax, and vocabulary on the other, really can tell teachers or their students how concepts in a written composition connect or fail to connect.

Seen generally, then, extant measures fail in very distinct ways to measure language performance, particularly the kind of performance that is represented in a network transcript. None of these measures looks at individual clause units (not just sentences, which may be composed of several clauses). None measures clauses according to their content as effective speech acts—as statements whose surface language forms convey topics and comments (and hence weight them for effectiveness and a kind of situational cogency rather than a more surface correctness). None weights concepts according to their logical cogency. Finally, these measures do not provide an objective means to assess an essay's strategic cohesion (explicit linguistic control of rhetorical features that express intent) in a way that teachers of writing and teachers of language would both acknowledge. The question of linguistic performance, then, must be rethought: teachers of grammar ought to be able to score essays in ways compatible with teachers of essay-writing, and researchers ought to be able to offer teachers clarification of their clear sense about beautiful paragraphs that say nothing, or poorly-articulated, yet idea-rich statements. These grey areas of assessment are shared by researchers and teachers, and are met with almost daily in student linguistic production at intermediate levels.

Since research about writing informs teaching practices, we therefore need diagnostic measures sensitive to improvement on the microlevels: in addition to being able to evaluate expanded *content* (idea units) and sentence *quantity,* as well as more accurate *morphosyntactic and organizational structures*, we need to diagnose whether individual written *concepts* become more cogent (appropriate, rhetorically-sophisticated, articulate) under various practice conditions. The following sections offer a suggestion to fill that need: a description and example of strategy coding as an assessment measure that can accommodate both research and teaching.

Criteria For Assessing Concepts

What does it mean for an assessment measure to rate strategic language management? To begin, the system must identify discrete strategy types—discriminate between various propositions or concepts that drive various kinds of language expression. Second, the coding must identify syntactic and semantic features that reflect a logical hierarchy in which a speech act is embedded, that is, the various possible relationships between surface language and the thought expressed or hidden in that language (its ideational intent). Third, coding must be sensitive to ideational relationships at the intersentential level, not just to discourse markers. In other words, not only local-level semantic and morphosyntactic relationships, but also larger discourse patterns (e.g., how topics are developed within a paragraph), must be reflected in coding criteria.

To further exemplify this thinking about strategy types in a discourse-sensitive system, consider a statement such as "we cannot read popular novels for new ideas," which is, in isolation, an *opinion* about popular literature. This same statement, however, exhibits a different strategic management when it occurs at the end of an essay that has documented the ways in which characters, social dynamics, and plot development differ in popular love stories, on the one hand, and *Madame Bovary* or *Jane Eyre*, on the other. When it sums up such an analysis, the statement "we cannot read popular novels for new ideas" draws a conclusion following the comparison of two unlike entities. There is an implicit cohesion between this sentence's idea and what went before, an assumed "therefore" or "it follows then" (Halliday, 1985). Relocated in the discourse, then, what on the surface seems to be an opinion has become a *causal proposition*.

How can the same surface language function in two ways? The answer here is similar to the answer that applies to speech acts. Discourse and context conditions change meaning. A popular movie titled *Honey, I Blew Up the Kids* similarly reframes a potential tragedy into a comedy. The semantics of "blew up" change from a field reflecting destruction by explosion to that of photographic enlargement to giant proportions ("the incredible colossal kids"), yielding amusing sequences in which toddlers terrify grown-ups with larger-than-life toddler behavior. The language of the title alone is insufficient to explain the basis for this movie's humor. We need the American context to understand the conceit on which its comparative code-switch is based: toddlers as loose cannons in their parents' lives—usually causing metaphoric, not physical explosions.

To return to the previous example, when a writer has compared two distinct entities (such as specific popular works and classical love stories), s/he has evaluated two alternative realities. Consequently, the original opinion clause, "we cannot read popular novels for new ideas," understood in this specific discourse context, proposes a new idea that follows from the writer's arguments, a conclusion drawn from the preceding comparison. In this context, it is no longer an opinion. At this point, slippage occurs in ways that the traditional coding options mentioned above do not accommodate.

The coding system that follows tries to remedy these lacunae by reflecting the insights of language theorists such as Wittgenstein who assert that meaningful writing consists of statements whose messages are created by their relationships to one another. Their meaning depends on text-internal (i.e., discursive or ideational), not text-external context (i.e., sociological or linguistic). A networking writer exhibits control of a discourse when his text-internal meaning becomes the site of discussion by others. Regardless of external contexts (e.g., whether fellow classmates have read *Madame Bovary* or not), the writer's context, because it is unambiguously signaled, sets the boundaries for discussion.

Coding Strategy Types by Clause

The coding system outlined below assumes that clauses generally serve one of four strategic options in a discourse:

- a purely *descriptive assertion* of fact
- an *opinion,* drawn from the speaker/writer's experience about the human condition and couched in *ad hominem* generalities
- an *evaluative claim,* which is anchored in a specified context or particular situation; often explicit comparisons or contrasts between two distinct entities
- a *causal conclusion* or new idea that follows from or is the result of a state of affairs on which an assertion, opinion or an evaluative claim (such as a comparison or contrast) is based

These categories are used as a base line against which a rater may begin to identify and evaluate surface language. How does a rater identify them? Let us look at the strategy types in order of their increasing logical complexity and in terms of the way surface features of language tag a particular logic.

1. Descriptions

Many descriptions can be readily distinguished from opinions by surface features. Descriptive clauses present what are commonly-held or easily-verifiable facts and therefore rely heavily on the verb "to be" and action verbs ("he goes to the store" or "she sings today"). Decisions about clauses with negation, however, tend to be resolved by discursive context. Thus "he never goes to the store" may well be a valid description of a bed-ridden individual or someone with a store phobia. In the context of a person complaining about lack of cooperation from a roommate in maintaining a household, however, the statement conveys an opinion (a covert complaint).

2 and 3. Opinions Or Claims Versus Evaluative Clauses

Both opinions and evaluative clauses can be preceded by a dummy clause such as: "I must say," "we believe that. . . ," "He is convinced that . . ." The difference between an opinion and an evaluative clause that contains these opionions will be the difference between a general claim about the speaker / writer's experience (outside the "text" of the immediate situational encounter) and a claim anchored in a specific reality whose reference suggests the clause that follows (a text- or situation-internal context). Therefore, opinions stand alone. Evaluative clauses necessitate discursive linking, even if not explicit grammatical links.

Compare, for example, the clauses in the following two sentences: "I think that American housewives watch too many soap operas," and "I think that when people talk about soap operas, they refer to daytime serials rather than to nighttime series."[3] The opinion about housewives and soap operas suggests neither a necessary follow-up (a line that must follow for the statement to make sense to a hearer / reader), nor any information drawn specifically from the discourse in progress. To be sure, the writer might go on to question his / her own veracity ("But is that true?") or offer another opinion ("I think soap operas are a waste of time."). In another way, such assertions break cohesion (talk about soap operas) by introducing a new dimension in the conversational flow ("me"). They interrupt the discourse context by intruding a personal opinion into the context of a language exchange.

In contrast to this assertion, the second example sentence, "I think that when people talk about soap operas, they refer to daytime serials rather than to nighttime series," sets the stage for a subsequent one; it leads the reader to expect a follow-up evaluation or a rationale for the evaluation, not just any kind of next clause as an expansion to the discourse. The reader anticipates a new insight, such as a claim that nighttime series have all the features of daytime soaps. Indeed, not only the next sentence, but the writer's discursive intent, is implied by the statement "I think that when people talk about soap operas, they refer to daytime serials rather than nighttime series." Some readers may anticipate an attack on, others at least an analysis of nighttime programming in, network television.

Thus, some discursive coherence may be implied by an opinion that is never made explicit or pursued within the discourse—we clearly understand that there are a limited number of options as follow-up, but have no discourse signals to anticipate what they are. In contrast with opinion clauses, then, an evaluative clause must either support a claim by a restriction unique to a particular situation (people refer only to daytime serials) or compare two distinct entities that figure in the evolving discourse (people refer to daytime serials, not nighttime series). In either case, an expansion of a unique discourse situation is created, a discursive context that is a discrete subset of general reality.

In contrast, the student who writes "soap operas are a waste of time" has neither restricted nor compared or contrasted her claim about the generic categories "soap operas" (the topic) and the fact that they are a waste of time (the comment); at best, she has tagged it as her own personal opinion by adding "I think." In contrast, the student who writes "soap operas/ that deal with pseudo-social problems/ are a waste of time" has restricted the topic by adding a qualifier. The type of soap opera under discussion now has specific frame of reference—those that deal with pseudo-social problems—and *is trying to control a discursive environment, not only react in general terms that might apply to virtually any context the speaker/ writer is in.*

Such discursive restrictions can frame comments as well as topics. The opinion "soap operas are a waste of time" becomes an evaluation when qualified by "for people who want to learn something." Instead of equating soap operas with a waste of time (without justifying that claim), soap operas are contrasted with learning in concrete terms. Only in the evaluative clauses is the verbal logic behind the opinion ("soap operas are a waste of time") explicitly linked to particular people or situations, through various grammatical, syntactical, or rhetorical gambits—only through such markers does the semantic reference for the words of a sentence become discourse-internal instead of dependent uniquely on the writer / speaker's location.

Because of such markers, readers know the basis for the writer's opinion and the point of view from which that base information is considered. With reference to a specified context, recipients of such a discourse can agree or disagree on a substantive rather than purely speculative basis. With a shared discursive context (like the one evolving on a network, for example, or in a shared communicative situation in an oral classroom), a greater likelihood exists that students will gradually try to develop ideas rather than engage in phatic exchanges of generic opinion.

Thus in response to the evaluative claim that one cannot learn anything from soap operas, a student on a network might appropriately respond, "I disagree. I learned a lot about divorce law from *As the World Turns*." This student's specification "about divorce law" qualifies the comment "learned a lot." With such an assertion, the respondent also implies that she is willing to pursue the topic "divorce law" on *As the World Turns*. In contrast, the response "I learned a lot from *As the World Turns*" would be an opinion, allowing responses to go in all directions. The qualification "about divorce law," then, raises the clause to the level of strategy evaluation, a necessary precursor to developing analytic argument and, not incidentally, raising the level of discourse complexity in which students engage.

4. Causal Propositions

If evaluative clauses anchor claims by restricting their scope through qualifications, explicit contrasts, or comparisons, then causal clauses introduce new ideas that follow from evaluative statements. Logically, causal clauses often follow no more than one descriptive or opinion clause, often in forms like "if-then," "because," "nonetheless," and "therefore."[4]

That claim has significant implications for writers and definitions of effectively managed discourse, for it implies that, under most writing conditions, descriptive and opinion clauses function largely as place markers within an overriding rhetorical and discursive development—they cannot be adequately defined in isolation. Factual statements by themselves lead nowhere. Similarly, unsupported opinions lack direction. *Only discursively-connected statements allow the writer/speaker to control the utterance.* It follows, then, that minimizing the frequency of unsupported assertions or opinions should lead to more compelling written expression.

The illustration provided here compares short statements made in response to a teacher's instructions on the network, not conversational gambits characteristic of many computer exchanges. The principles of assessment are, however, equally applicable to those exchanges. Students or teachers, once familiar with the coding system, can read networking transcripts to identify the degree of discursive management or control exhibited by participants in a class conducted along the lines of a more conversation-like exchange. The system can, then, be used in two ways: 1) by teachers to measure progress of writers in strategic management of discourse, and 2) by students to raise their consciousness about strategies that result in greater control of their written expression. In either case, as will be demonstrated below, the coding is not time-consuming and requires no special expertise. Hence it is a convenient tool for both self-monitoring and evaluation purposes.

Weighting Strategy Types: Evolving Scoring Criteria

The foregoing section has described strategies exhibited in clauses and emphasized the distinction between rhetorically open-ended statements (descriptions and general opinions) with statements that are text-specific (evaluative and causal assertions). The illustrations of coding emphasize that only evaluative and causal assertions control discourse direction. And although two major types of discourse emerge (text-neutral versus text-specific statements), their weighting within a strategy coding system needs further differentiation. The following section of this discussion explores the weighting of propositions realized as grammatical clauses, as such weighting is a function of discourse complexity. This weighting also argues for a five-part scale that would be appropriate to both teaching and research contexts, rewarding unintelligible statements or misfires with no points, descriptions (as simple sentences, no matter how many clauses they contain) with one point, opinions with two points, evaluative clauses (which represent synthetic reasoning expanding on discourse propositions) with three points, and causal clauses (which both analyze the relationship between discourse and context, and synthesize statements) four points.

1. Discursive considerations

The rationale behind lower point values given to descriptive and opinion clauses than to evaluative and causal clauses is as follows. As already stated, strategies for topics and comments in descriptive and opinion clauses apply discourse-external contexts. Either the real world or an imagined actuality is described, but without initiating control or direction specific to the evolving written text. While descriptive clauses may be chained as in the *nouveau roman* ("He walked into the garden. He bent to pick a flower."), each sentence could also stand alone without altering its descriptive function to any great degree. The hearer / reader is left guessing how and if these statements are to be added up into the speaker / writer's point of view. That speaker / writer is thus not really in control of the discourse, they are exploiting it.

Similarly, opinions can be chained in discourse ("You're so vain. You're always looking in the mirror. You think nobody matters but you"), but like descriptive clauses, such opinions are just as valid in isolation as in the discourse chain. Again, differences, if any, involve intensified, not modified meaning—they do not evolve; at best, they introduce emotional color.

Opinions are, then, undistinguished by significant reference to a specific context created within the text. Carly Simon's song / opinion "You're So Vain" may imply qualifications about Mick Jagger's personality, but not until the song's referent (evaluative) clause comes up ("I bet you think this song is about you") does the first statement's implication become concrete accusation, implying a discrete relationship between two parties. The vain person at issue is generic until restricted by an explicit comparison between generic vanity and particular behavior characterizing his / her vanity.

Unlike descriptions and opinions, neither evaluative nor causal clauses can have a full life of their own outside their discursive context. If the evaluative "I bet you think this song is about you" is extrapolated from Carly Simon's song, its qualifying function is lost. All by itself, the assertion becomes a different statement with a different rhetorical function. In other words, without reference to preceding claims, the clause turns into a generic statement of opinion. Consequently, the strategy of evaluative statements emerges only within a specific discourse. By extension, the same point carries for causal propositions. Defined as concepts that present new ideas following from preceding conclusions drawn, causal propositions too are necessarily discourse-dependent (there are no generic "becauses" except in conversations with recalcitrant toddlers).

2. *Formal Considerations In Scoring*

Due to their fluidity in the total discourse structure, sentences evaluated as strategic clauses cannot be strictly characterized by their morphosyntax, as has already been argued. Nonetheless, the trajectory for increasing complexity moves from factual assertions, to opinions, to evaluations, and, ultimately, to causal propositions—and as these strategies move towards logically more complex attempts to manage the information in a discourse situation, they will *require* (not only give the option for) more complex syntax.

Descriptive statements generally involve the simplest morphosyntax in any language: subjects, action verbs or the verb to be, and a limited range of choices among verbal complements, objects, indirect objects, and objects of prepositions. Opinions add to these such options as the use of negation, modals, and subordinate clauses, often with "that" or relative pronouns as conjunctions, that anchor opinion in a particular perspective (I think, see, presume, and so on).

To restrict, compare, or contrast, the evaluative and causal clause types tend to add information by adding syntactic complexity: embeddings, relative clauses, or subordinate clauses that qualify, elaborate, deny, or attribute. Evaluative and causal clauses are frequently marked by subordinating or coordinating conjunctions and a range of adverbial markers. Take, as an example of complexity, the statement: "Because nighttime series present the same problems as daytime serials [evaluative claim, chaining up individual information the evolving discourse], the difference between the two is in scheduling only [causal claim, adding external information to expand the discourse context and direction of the further discussion]."

But note that complex sentence constructions, while more likely, are not necessary for a discourse to reflect cognitive complexity. Some very good native speakers develop complex evaluative or causal arguments in elegant and compelling English using simple Subject-Verb-Object sentences (e.g., "we cannot dedicate, we cannot consecrate, we cannot hallow this ground"). Formal structure alone does not determine a clause's strategic content. Thus, in the foregoing example about soap operas, one might find a variant expressing the ideas noted above without subordination, yet revealing the same logic: "Nighttime series present the same problems as daytime serials [evaluative clause]. In a real sense, the only difference between the two is one of scheduling [causal clause]."

3. Weighting Considerations

As the foregoing argues, the system of awarding point values that is being evolved here attempts to reward logical cogency within a discourse. As already indicated, neither descriptions nor opinions contribute, in and of themselves, to logical development of ideas. Hence they rank numerically lower than evaluative (comparison) and causal clauses—they are of higher cognitive complexity, reflecting a more complex sense about the speaker/writer's possibility and ability to control the discourse or communicative situation.

Similarly, between the two lower-ranked clause types, opinion clauses tend to access more complex linguistic structures than mere descriptions, even though they do not absolutely require them, if the speaker/hearer is clever at chaining up simple sentences in ways that imply much more than they state explicitly. Hence, they are awarded two points, one point higher than simple descriptive statements. Their higher value is not given for grammaticality by itself, however. The more complex structures in judgmental thinking are presumed to indicate that the writer is one step further on the road toward the more complex conceptualization involved in reasoned argumentation than the student who relies more heavily on descriptive clauses. To receive the points, the form of a clause must correspond to its discursive purpose which is the overriding factor in its scoring—it must further the type of communication that is being pursued.

Evaluations, as necessary preconditions for developing ideas, represent the first state in logical argument. They are points A and B in syllogistic reasoning: "All soap operas deal with exaggerated problems. Many nighttime series present related traumatic situations week after week." Point C is made when the causal inference to an evaluative statement becomes explicit. This particular syllogism is completed by an inference such as: "Therefore many nighttime series are soap operas by another name." This writer has taken decisive control of the discussion and furthered it.

In sum, to differentiate between the discursive, linguistic, and logical complexities involved in using the four clausal categories, the following point values were assigned: one point for descriptive clauses, two points for opinions, three points for evaluative clauses, and four points for causal clauses.

In two cases, it is possible for a rater or teacher to award no points at all. First, where clauses present redundant information that does not promote idea development or rhetorical intensification, they receive zero points. Second, where clauses prove unintelligible to a sympathetic reader (one sensitive to L2 articulation problems and the discursive flow of the text), zero points are given. Such an option balances length with meaningful discursive content. In this sense, then, the scale has five point values.

Sample Weighting of Two Paragraphs

To illustrate diagnostic procedures in this scoring system, two writing samples produced during a computer network session will now be scored.[5] Both paragraphs were written by the same student in a fifth-semester German class. That student's class met once weekly in the computer lab and undertook a variety of tasks, one of which was writing one or two paragraphs at the outset of the computer session. Students were to elaborate a point of view in these paragraphs or short essays and send them on the network. These short texts, in turn, were read by classmates who would comment on them in exchanges on the network that took up the rest of the class hour. The samples presented here have been translated into English for the convenience of readers unfamiliar with the German language (see the Appendices for the German originals). Some effort has been made to transliterate grammaticality and intelligibility features of the originals.

The first paragraph was drawn from week two and the second from week fifteen of a fifteen-week semester. The German originals reveal about the same number of morphosyntactic errors. The second paragraph reveals greater continuity and would presumably get higher marks in global scoring for organization or coherence, yet such a score would probably reveal little to the student about what kind of improvements have been made or need to be made. The student's conscious control of this discourse would remain a nebulous macro-factor of the communicative situation rather than a consistent pattern at the micro- or clausal level. Because strategic scoring pinpoints processes that either promote or discourage coherent discourse, this assessment measure provides tangible indices about organization and content of written work.

The first sample, produced during the second week of class, was written after viewing an episode of the popular nighttime soap opera *Dynasty* in German:

I must say I find soap operas a curse on humanity. But the Television is the greatest curse and I always watch TV. The soap opera is nonetheless the worst, because they are so addictive. One thought, that one always has to go home and look at the last program. But I don't understand, why these programs have to be so absurd. How many businesses can one person have?

Strategy Scoring Of Essay #1

Clausal propositions	Evaluation
C 1* I must say** I find soap operas a curse on humanity.	2 points—a general opinion
C2 But the Television is the greatest curse	2 points—a general opinion
C3 and I always watch TV.	1 point—general description
C4 The soap opera is nonetheless the worst,	2 points—a general opinion
C4 because they are so addictive.	3 points—qualifies soap operas
C5 One thought,** that one always has to go home	2 points—makes a claim about contingent necessity
C6 in order to look at the last program [the latest episode].	4 points—causal relationship to preceding claim, presents contingency
C7 But I don't understand,** why these programs have to be so absurd.	2 points—a general observation
C8 How many businesses can one person have?	1 point—general description

* C = clause

** "I must say", "one thought", and "I don't understand" are not coded since they only mark perspective and serve no predictive function

The statement in sample #1 has eight clauses, in the sense defined above. Total points are eighteen. When total points are divided by the number of clauses, this essay reveals a 2.2 average of strategic complexity.

The following paragraph was written fourteen weeks later by the same student. The class had, prior to this point in the semester, viewed popular German language television programs from different genres (romance, fables, and adventure series) and read both popular and serious literatures in these three genres. They were asked during the networking session in the last week of class to reflect about the differences between "high" and "low" culture texts:

> I believe that the difference between popular literature and serious literature is not very large. It could be, when one compares the two, that they are both very similar. "All Quiet on the Western Front" and "Starship Enterprise" can be concerned with a similar problem, but I believe that there are other problems, that the trivial literature cannot address, because this style is often so simplistic. The opinion [intentionality] is often lost in the text.

Clausal propositions	Evaluation
C1 I believe that the difference between popular literature and serious literature is not very large.	3 points—an explicit comparison between two distinct entities
C2 It could be, when one compares the two, that they are both very similar.	2 points—an opinion. The embedded "when one compares the two" brings no new information
C3 "All Quiet on the Western Front" and "Starship Enterprise" can be concerned with a similar problem,	3 points—qualified by the similar problem, a comparison is possible
C4 but I believe that there are other problems that the trivial literature cannot address,	3 points—an exclusionary restriction that leads to contrast
C5 because this style is often so simplistic.	3 points—specifies the basis for the exclusionary restriction in C4
C6 The opinion [intentionality] is often lost in the text.	4 points—a new idea (i.e., trivial literature is not in control of its message systems) follows from the evaluative logic in clauses 4 and 5

This paragraph also has an eighteen point total in strategic complexity, but only six clauses coded. Thus simple division yields a 3.0 average complexity, a gain of .8 over the paragraph written earlier in the semester.

What does this measure say about the student's progress? Both samples were produced in a non-controlled situation. Students were instructed only to write what they thought, and spent some time reading each other's comments. As comparison between the English translations and the unedited German language samples suggests (see the Appendices), grammaticality has not improved and sentence length has actually declined.

Yet to say just that to a student as an evaluation is in many ways inadequate, since the second sample shows a clear kind of growth: the student is trying to manage the discourse in more strategic and sophisticated ways, not just react to questions. Neither pure grammaticality nor length suffices as a measure against which to comment on writing conducted on a computer network, since effective, spontaneous communication was sought, not necessarily length, absolute grammaticality, or evidence of rewriting. The strategy scoring, on the other hand, is more appropriate to this second task, because it uncovers another dimension of a writer's ability to develop a discourse-specific logic in an immediate communicative setting. And, by that measure, this student reveals greater control in essay two as regards the content and direction of written expression. What a teacher would instinctively feel about an appropriate comparison of these two passages has been recovered as an empirical measure that may be replicated without prior knowledge of the student, as well.

Conclusion

In exploring the strategy measurement outlined above and the uses of its scoring (also potentially for the classroom), the objective of this chapter has been to illustrate the use of a diagnostic tool. No specific claims can be made about students' gains through networking on the basis of the brief examples provided here.

Rather, a case is made for an analytical measure that reflects strategic control of discourse. By implication however, this measure is linked to presumptions about the specific benefits of networking, as described in other chapters of this volume. In fact, the whole idea of coding concepts came after reading fifteen weeks of student exchanges and recognizing a developmental pattern that pointed to increasingly cogent language interaction. It seemed essential, then, that a system be devised to register the micro-elements of directed versus nebulous communication.

The coding system presented here suggests that a more extended, controlled study of student achievement using this measure would be looking for precisely the communicative gains presumed by many authors in this volume. Moreover, while the affective responses documented here are valuable in and of themselves, teachers of composition will need also to assess how composition skills (that is, skills for managing more complex communication situations, orally or in writing) develop among students engaged in networking.

Clearly, then, studies comparing progress between traditional classes and networking classes in identical curricula will need to be undertaken. Increasingly, for example, researchers are exploring writing from a variety of perspectives: not only structural accuracy or organization as such, but also how students feel about writing and what kinds of writing they are able to undertake successfully. Performance goals (such as the ability to write for different audiences or adapt what has been learned in class to real-world settings) will also need to be measured to identify whether what is learned has practical application. Assessing concepts, as has been outlined above, would help to identify discourse control within such specific communication situations, a significant feature of effective written expression.

The concept coding presented here was thus also developed as a response to the interactions found in a networking class for the students' benefit. It was used to illustrate to students how they might communicate more effectively, how to develop a monitor for rhetorical / logical cohesion that can aid them in sorting out the origin of grammaticality problems. This chapter has explored perspectives yielded by assessing concepts. I have argued that since conventional assessments fail to measure the gap between linguistic and organizational competence on the one hand and strategic competence of a student on the other, such a measure is needed. Since this problem plagues both first and second-language composition classes, then, these suggestions are intended for both audiences.

Appendix A

Original German-Language Writing Samples (with original errors)

#1
Ich muß sagen, daß ich finde Seifenopern ein Fluch an Humanitat. Aber der Fernseher ist das großte Fluch, und ich sehe immer Fern. Die Seifenopern ist jedoch die schlechtes, weil sie so addiktive sind. Man dachte, daß man muß immer nach Hause gehen um die letzte Sendung zu sehen. Aber ich verstehe nicht, warum diese Sendungen so absurd sein müssen. Wieviele Geshäfte kann ein Person haben?

#2
Ich glaube, daß der Unterschied zwishen trivialer Literatur und ernster Literature nicht so groß ist. Es könnte sein, wenn man die zwei vergleicht, daß die beiden sehr gleich sind. "Im Westen Nichts Neues" und "Raumschiff Enterprise" können sich um ein ähnliches Problem handeln, aber ich glaube, daß es gibt andere Probleme, die der triviale Literatur nicht addressieren kann, weil diese Stil oft so simplistisch ist. Die Meinung ist oft im Text verloren.

Appendix B

Mark Willard:
Ich glaube, daß der Unterschied zwishen trivialer Literatur und ernster Literature nicht so groß ist. Es könnte sein, wenn man die zwei vergleicht, daß die beiden sehr gleich sind. "Im Westen Nichts Neues" und "Raumschiff Enterprise" können sich um ein ähnliches Problem handeln, aber ich glaube, daß es gibt andere Probleme, die der triviale Literatur nicht addressieren kann, weil diese Stil oft so simplistisch ist. Die Meinung ist oft im Text verloren.

Denise Lami:
Was ist die Unterschieden zwischen die Boulevardliteratur und die Literatur? Ich glaube sie sind klar als das Glas. Boulevardliteratur hat keine relative Informationen für den intelligenten Leuten, und im Gegenteil kann man von der Literatur viele Informationen zu benutzen, deshalb liegt die Literatur auf einer höher Ebene.

Robert Lee Stanley:

Der Hauptünterschied zwischen die triviale Literatur und die ernste Literatur ist für mich eine Sache von Charakturen. Der Denver Clan, Mit dem Sturm Kam die Liebe, und das Raumschiff Enterprise haben alle einfache Charakturen mit nur einer Dimension. Ich interessiere mich nicht für solche Texen. Lieber habe ich Die Leiden des jungen Werthers, Tatort, und Im Westen Nichts Neues, insofern als die tiefere Charakturen haben. Mit der ernsten Literatur kann man viel mehr sehen, zum Beispiel wie oft und wie viel man mit selbst kämpft. Die Charakturen der triviale Literatur kämpfen am meisten mit anderen Charakturen oder kämpfen darum, daß die einer höchen und stereotypicshen Purpose dienen. Zum genauen Beispiel, Kapitän Picard dient den

Greg M Crowe:

Ich denke, daB die Probleme heute in Los Angeles nicht vermieden werden können, weil die Polizisten, die Rodney King so schwer und lang geschlagt haben, nicht im Gefängnis sind. Da sie frei sind, sieht es aus, als ob sie absolut nichts gegen den Gesellschaft gemacht haben. Meiner Meinung nach sind diese Männer sehr schlechte Verbrechern, insofern als sie den Gesellschaft schützen sollen. Aber jetzt können die L.A. Polizei nicht getraut werden. Die Einwohner in Los Angeles wollen, daB die Polizei mit diesem Unsinn aufhören werden. Sie beschweren sich viel über diese Situation. Obwohl die Leute, die in süd L.A. wohen, sich an dieser Situation gewöhnt haben, sind sie müde von sie. Diese arme, schwarze Leute haBen die weiBe Polizei, die immer schwarze Männer schlecht behandeln, und sie sind verrückt gegangen und haben viel von den Geschäften gestöhlen, nachdem die weiBe Polizei, die Feinde gegen die schwarze Leute sind, frei gegangen sind. Jetzt kämpfen alle die schwarze Leute in L.A. gegen weiBe Leute. Ein paar wieBe Leute sind von ihren Autos gerriBt und schwer geschlagt.

Kimberly Lynn Bartlett:

Thema: der vergleich zwischen deutche abenteuerenfilmen wie Tatort und amerikanischen abenteuerenfilm

Ich finde, daß der Unterschied von den deutchen und amerikanischen abenteueren Filmen sind sehr weit insofern als der deutchen Filmen nicht zu häßlich. Zum Beispiel Tatort, der ein berühmste deutche abenteurere Sendung ist, gibt man eine komplizierte Handlung mit weniger Blüt und gewaltätigkeit als die amerikanischen. Während ein Programm oder ein Film von die USA, findet man gute Handlung und Geschichte aber auch bald kommt die Gewalt.

References

Brown, J. D. (1991). Do English and ESL faculties rate writing samples differently? *TESOL Quarterly, 25*, 587-603.

Carrell, P. L., & Connor, U. (1991). Reading and writing descriptive and persuasive texts. *Modern Language Journal, 75*, 314-24.

Celce-Murcia, M. (1991). Grammar pedagogy in second and foreign language teaching." *TESOL Quarterly, 25*, 459-80.

Fathman, A. K., & Whalley, E. (1990). "Teacher response to student writing: Focus on form versus content." In B. Kroll (Ed.), *Second language writing: Research insights for the classroom* (pp. 178-190). Cambridge: Cambridge University Press.

Halliday, M. A. K. (1985). *An introduction to functional grammar.* London: Edward Arnold.

Horowitz, D. M. (1986). What professors actually require. Academic tasks in the ESL classroom. *TESOL Quarterly, 20*, 445-62.

Kepner, C. G. (1991). An experiment in the relationship of types of written feedback to the development of second-language writing skills. *Modern Language Journal, 75*, 305-24.

Kroll, B. (Ed.) (1990). *Second language writing: Research insights for the classroom.* Cambridge: Cambridge University Press.

Larsen-Freeman, D., & Long, M. (1991). *An introduction to second language acquisition research.* New York: Longman.

Parrish, B., & Tarone, E. (1986). Article use in interlanguage: A study in task-related variability. Paper presented at the TESOL Convention, Anaheim, CA.

Perkins, K. (1983). On the use of composition scoring techniques: Objective measures and objective tests to evaluate ESL writing ability. *TESOL Quarterly, 17*, 651-71.

Raimes, A. (1991). Out of the woods. Emerging traditions in the teaching of writing. *TESOL Quarterly, 25*, 407-30.

Santos, T. (1989). Replication in applied linguistics research. *TESOL Quarterly, 23*, 699-702.

Santos, T. (1991). Review of *Second language writing: Research insights for the classroom. TESOL Quarterly, 25*, 710-14.

Schaughnessy, M. P. (1977). *Errors and expectations.* New York: Oxford University Press.

Shohamy, E., Gordon, C. M., & Kraemer, R. (1992). The effect of raters' background and training on the reliability of direct writing tests. *Modern Language Journal, 76*, 27-33.

Searle, J. (1969). *Speech acts.* Cambridge: Cambridge University Press.

Toulmin, S. E. (1958). *The uses of argument.* New York: Cambridge University Press.

Notes

[1]Although the present analysis looks at a writing sample in a second language, the principles behind the assessments illustrated here do have crossover potential for assessing samples written in a first language.

[2]Rhetorical control as used here refers to control of the global arrangement or organization of a text in order to address a particular audience and achieve particular ends. In many cases, however, rhetorical control encompasses the morphosyntactic as well as the discursive issues addressed here. To avoid confusion about possible conflating of linguistic and discursive features, this paper uses the concept "strategic discourse management" as a subset of the more encompassing entity "rhetorical control."

[3]These examples are translated from a German-language transcript of a student discussion about soap-operas on the InterChange computer network (see Appendix).

[4]Note that some of these are conjunctions and some are adverbs, just reconfirming the various relationships between the meaning of a sentence proposition and the words used to express that meaning.

[5]No experimental claims are made here since neither an outside control group nor cohorts within class were established prior to analysis of these. The samples used here are drawn from a set of statements about the same topic and chosen at random from the available student pool. In both cases writing was in spontaneous (i.e., unprepared) response to the instructions of the teacher at the outset of a computer networking class.

Towards the Future: Suggestions for Research and the Classroom

Janet Swaffar

The chapters in this volume have focused on computer use in real expression as contrasted with display writing (e.g., Horowitz, 1986). Fundamental to this project has been the conviction that enabling practice in real expression is one of the most effective ways to help students improve their writing by formal as well as expressive standards. In conjunction with that insight has been the related conviction that *the networking experience of first- and second- language teachers is mutually informing*. We have more to learn from one another than is currently acknowledged.

As the essays document, particularly those by Chun, Kelm, Markley, and Sullivan, students who network, whether in a first or second language, are students who write to communicate and exchange their views. In this sense, networking contrasts with usual classroom practice in any language class, where writing tends to focus on practice in learning a formal standard. Success or failure in such a setting is more likely to be normed linguistically, not on the basis of how effectively students exchange and develop ideas. Thus, networking provides a medium that enables teachers to facilitate their students' exchange of ideas in a manner quite different from that characteristic in the more traditional writing classroom. When writing tasks are assigned in most classes, students produce papers outside of class; their writing goal is to "display" sample work that will meet linguistic and conceptual standards set by the teacher (Raimes, 1991).

Most networking situations described in studies such as those in this volume almost preclude such display behaviors because synchronous writing assignments on a network have students, not teachers, establish communicative standards. Students, more often than teachers, ask each other "what do you mean by . . . ?" In addition, concurrent discourses promote spontaneous interaction. By format alone, teacher-controlled, sequential discourses (writing to be read as self-referential assertions) open fewer avenues for free expression of ideas. At the same time, teacher monitoring and guidance is essential, or networking becomes an end in itself, lacking the structure needed to achieve specific educational goals. As a guided exercise, however, networking can structure synchronous, concurrent discourses. Elaboration, modification, and self-correction seem to be typical behaviors in this environment. By fostering writing as a developmental process, from initial stages toward a final written product, a networked classroom can provide an intermediary step between display and "real" writing, serving as a microcosm of what should happen in a student's real-world essay writing or written argumentation.

Since a common thread among the chapters presented here is the importance of teacher structuring in a networking class, what follows is a synthesis of suggestions for classroom use at various learning levels. Characteristic for all these suggestions is Markley's caveat about the need for teacher management. While instructors will not be a major visible presence in network transcripts as students progress in their language learning, the teacher's covert role as decision-makers about the tasks undertaken during the class hour is no less a planning requirement than would be the case in a traditional classroom. Unlike the teachers and classes in the traditional classroom, however, the InterChange teachers and their classes have transcripts and access to programs that help them assess various aspects of performance on those transcripts. Hence clear instructional expectations become essential if students are to perceive InterChange work as integral to their progress in a course and if teachers are going to be able to assess those transcripts as evidence of that progress.

These expectations need not be elaborate. A simple verbal or posted assignment at the outset of class ("Today I am asking you to . . ." or "I will be reading transcripts for at least two to three examples of . . . .") may suffice. Other instructors may wish to specify participation on the course syllabus as numerical credit for presence and a minimum number of entries per session. The point here is not necessarily the form of stated expectations but that these expectations be explicit and clear to participants at all times. InterChange, the networking program used by many of the classes discussed here, is a pleasurable experience, but it must also be pedagogically structured in ways that motivate and reward participation that individual teachers consider valuable.

The following considerations are important for the discussion below. Students just learning a foreign language have special needs distinct from those of students performing tasks in their native tongue. Therefore, practices typical for English composition students will be different from those for students in beginning and second-year language classes. However, the implications for English composition of the practices used in advanced foreign language classes strongly suggest potential cross-fertilization between their pedagogies and philosophies of language and language learning, a basis for future bridges in research and across the curriculum.

Implementation in the Classroom

First semester foreign language students. Beginning language students will use InterChange primarily for practice of minimal language variations. With their highly restricted vocabulary, most beginner textbooks guide students toward practice expressing the content of inquiries about study or leisure plans, living arrangements, biographies or similar topics covered in their texts. The obvious advantage of InterChange is that it reinforces oral learning with practice in reading and writing, thus complementing the class conversations and small group work characteristic of most beginning language classes. As in the classroom, teachers can ask students to use the InterChange in conferencing among two or three students or to address the class as a whole. In either case, the class will have an opportunity to monitor their expressive abilities online and subsequently, as well, if printed transcripts are made available.

Aside from the motivational spur of computer use (e.g., Beauvois, Jaeglin this volume), opportunities for cleverness and experimentation abound. Initially, the verbal experiments of beginning learners will not be discursively correct, in the sense of standard usage, but they will enable students to be playful and enjoy using unfamiliar words to express familiar ideas. As Sullivan and Beauvois point out in their chapters, students like to ask each other personal questions and crack jokes, and they can do it in the "real time" networking offers. This spontaneity can be channeled in a variety of ways when the teacher keys attention differently: by subject matter ("talk about your favorite foods"), by grammatical feature ("check specifically for subject and verb agreement"), or even by rhetorical appropriateness ("address people you know only slightly"). Probably, however, the first transcripts will focus on conceptual or subject matter communication, a chiefly semantic practice for novice learners.

After a few weeks, and depending on analysis of InterChange transcripts, teachers may want to begin focusing attention on a particular morphosyntactic feature they consider vital to this stage in their students' competence to communicate in the language studied (e.g., pronouns and verb reference for Spanish, subject and verb agreement for German and French). Because writing allows for reflection and monitoring of tangible and recoverable data (words on a screen rather than transient speech), students can cross check their accuracy as a function of communicative clarity. For example, when students write "sie kommen zu spät" (instead of the third person "sie kommt") but are talking about a particular person, a question arises about whether the observer means "she" or "they." Often peers "correct" by simply inquiring about meaning (rather than form), but the end-effect is nonetheless grammar learning.

Teachers familiar with the ACTFL proficiency guidelines will note parallels between speech development categories at, for example, the novice, intermediate low, mid, or high levels and transcript performance as beginning students progress through the semester. If the University of Texas experience has validity in other institutional settings, however, teachers will find that student performance differs from the guidelines with respect to the rhetorical capabilities of their students. InterChange seems to facilitate discourse gambits. Hence earlier emphasis on the ability to mark, for example, contrast (but, however), chronology (afterwards, before), or causality (therefore, because) and to chain sentences in extended discourse will be more characteristic of the computer transcripts in our experience than seems to be true for classroom conversations (e.g., Chun, this volume). To confirm or disconfirm these suppositions, however, empirical research must be undertaken to compare actual progress in speaking and writing between a control group with oral conferencing and an InterChange class with parallel topical foci.

Second semester foreign language students. Due to students' general unfamiliarity with authentic speech acts, first semester work in foreign languages naturally stresses vocabulary practice and focus on grammar usage that inhibits exchanges of concrete information. By the second semester, however, particularly if class materials include authentic video and written texts, students have native-speaker models for connecting arguments or elaborating their ideas. Consequently, the network will probably reflect initial struggles to address larger content issues. At the same time, students must attempt to control unfamiliar and extremely limited vocabulary and grammar, characteristically with single sentences and relatively frequent Anglicisms or other native-language idioms. They will, nonetheless, experiment and work toward conceptual control of connected speech. Students begin to link ideas and chain a stream of sentences. Word order becomes more important as students strive to express subordinate and coordinate ideas overtly, experimenting with rhetorical markers such as adverbs or word order shifts for particular emphases. In German, for example, word order changes in coordinate and subordinate clauses or when adverbs are fronted. Control of these shifts signals effective exchanges. Depending on the language, then, such features may prompt teachers to alert students to rhetorical monitoring tasks either during networking or afterward (e.g., the teacher asks students to critique selected anonymous exchanges on printouts of transcript pages).

By the time students have progressed into their second year, their linguistic capabilities are poised to develop in a variety of directions. Networking activities will, then, depend upon particular course objectives stressed in a given institution. If preparing for foreign language use in interdisciplinary programs, students will want to practice conceptual empowerment—did they, for example, understand the ideas expressed in a Spanish language critique of the World Bank practices in Mexico or a French analysis of Terrorism in Algeria? Indeed, it may well be appropriate to use English to confirm student grasp of textual concepts.

If students are asked to write in the foreign language, however, teachers cannot anticipate displays of the morphosyntactic command these same students have when discussing events in their own lives or other concrete and student-referenced topics characteristic of most first year learning. The complexity of vocabulary and cognitive processing in such discussions renders such expectations unrealistic. Focus, then, should be on how learners progress in coherent (rather than precisely accurate) expression of thought when engaging in formal or complex cognitive tasks such as abstract thinking about unfamiliar situations conveyed in unfamiliar language. Both first- and second-language students can be formally and conceptually correct, without being rhetorically correct—signalling their speech acts with the appropriate markers for elaboration, contrast, qualification, and the like.

Conversely, if emphasis is on conversational command of language and accurate expository style, then the InterChange offers an ideal communicative and peer correction medium by means of which to strive for grammatical accuracy in tandem with rhetorical control. As in first year, the student is encouraged to be in charge of his or her accuracy goal. In this environment, that monitoring strategy can be framed as a particular focus for linguistic attention (e.g., "Today, monitor tense agreement among verbs as you discuss last summer's imaginary trip to Europe").

Various accuracy goals can also be linked to regular classroom reading assignments in a variety of ways, even in what seems to be an open discussion. By asking students to report on how they reacted to textual language (what they liked, didn't like, what was clear, unclear), teachers can solicit student responses to particular grammar features. Network activities can link comprehension checks and syntax when teachers select, for example, one or two complex clauses from the assigned reading and ask students to transform them into a series of simple ideas. Subsequent student comments on these transformations (what some extrapolated that others did not and linguistic or cohesive factors leading to ideas inferred) can confirm the inventory of textual concepts. Moreover, asking participants to compare reader responses to their transformations against the original, the instructor can highlight the function of subordination or embedding as a grammatical feature and a stylistic technique in the work read.

The options for grammar transformations that involve a stage between reproduction and language generation will depend on texts themselves and the teacher's perception of what students need to be able to do. Yet by asking network participants to alter textual aspect (from factual indicative to speculative subjunctive), voice (from third to first person), or time (from current to past) in a particular paragraph, instructors can introduce a straightforward grammar review that can also be the basis for related student comments about the impact of these changes on the ideas expressed in the original text.

Students in English composition and Upper Division foreign language courses. At this level, the overlap between foreign language learners and English composition students broadens. Students of English composition can benefit from networking in ways not dissimilar to the benefits available to advanced foreign language learners. Like native speakers of a language, foreign language majors and advanced students will be engaging in more language generation tasks than was practicable in their second year of study and approach the levels of tasks that English students engage in. Along with the foregoing suggestions, then, foreign language instructors will be designing activities to elicit paragraph length or even longer statements. Moreover, in contrast with less proficient students, these students can profitably be guided toward attempting reflective assessments.

Whereas second year foreign language students typically generate little more than connected descriptions and opinions, advanced students and native speakers of English are poised to undertake sophisticated arguments, assess what has been read or discussed and synthesize information and ideas in developed argument. Such undertakings will encourage students to reach beyond the purview of everyday speech into the realm of written discourse whose effectiveness rests on use of content, grammar, and rhetorical savvy.

This demanding synthesis of complex subject matter, performative context, and commensurately nuanced formal features is, in whatever language, fostered through the pre-writing activities—critical analysis and information exchanges—available through networking systems. Instructional guidance for networking among advanced students can, therefore, appropriately lead to pre-writing. In a networking environment, teachers can encourage students to try out tentative directions for papers, receive feedback, and, concomittantly, monitor the accuracy and rhetorical effectiveness of entries in the process.

Such emphases will stress the value of using assigned texts as the basis for InterChange elaborations. They will also introduce more advance preparation for initial entries on InterChange than was characteristic for Lower Division foreign language courses. Frequently, teachers of English composition or advanced foreign language courses specify networking tasks on syllabi so that students come to class prepared, be it to review of discourse markers, to comment on particular specialized texts or vocabulary or to elaborate on notations for short drafts that will be entered on the InterChange. Thus the students who have read about French and Algerian relations might be asked either on their assignment schedule or at the outset of class to "State the thesis of your paper—the role of France in Algeria's future and briefly illustrate what evidence supports your point of view"—a first stage in drafting a longer essay.

Phase two of that same class would ask students to compare what they have written with the versions presented by other students and to make appropriate comments. Such tasks will, as Markley's and Sullivan's chapters have indicated, elicit a variety of responses: Among them, praise, suggestions, elaborations, inquiries, and objections. The important factor, however, will be the group dynamic generated by open discussion. A student's writing task becomes an event initiating discussion rather than a monologue. Exchanges are folded into socialization and fostered by intense engagement with immediately available interlocutors.

Graduate students. Whereas networking has become relatively common for graduate courses in English composition, graduate instructors in foreign languages have, at the University of Texas, been more hesitant to adapt it into their curriculum. In large measure, this reluctance seems to stem from the culture of foreign language teaching at the graduate level, one that, for seminars, assumes a limited degree of verbal articulateness on the part of students and, for survey courses, still relies heavily on lecture formats. The idea of allotting class time from lectures to group discussion strikes some teachers as counterproductive. Similarly, they assume verbal discussion in seminars can facilitate communication more efficiently than can an InterChange discussion.

What is overlooked in such assumptions is the importance of enabling graduate students practice in gaining rhetorical control of the concepts central to their discipline and subdisciplines. Graduate students may be articulate in a foreign language, but most still need to learn how to talk about a problem in literary or linguistic analysis in terms of particular theoretical discourses within their discipline, whether that subfield is, for example, text-immanent interpretation or Universal Grammar. Additionally, many graduate students need to hone their foreign language skills in these specialized areas and will benefit from a demanding level of writing practice.

As a trial experience in using this technology, one graduate survey of modern German literature with fifteen students experimented with using the network regularly during the semester. The transcript language used alternated between German and English since the instructional goal was to enable students to learn strategies for interpretation by practicing a particular approach first in English and the subsequent week in German. Thus students could practice first in English the unfamiliar concepts and terminology of, for example, feminist theory, by looking for textual instances of gender dominance and its linguistic and social manifestation (who conflicts with whom, how, what happens as a result). In a subsequent week, with a different text, they would explore these same features using German terminology.

Asked for a written assessment of network use during the eighth week of the semester, all participants voted to continue the computer experience. Additionally, students stressed the value of making a transcript printout available outside of class so that they could further reflect about arguments and insights made during the class hour. Uniformly, these anonymous written comments emphasized the value of networking in fostering communication among class members, increasing their confidence about their ability to express themselves in German, and helping them think and write about literature in terms of different literary schools. Tentatively, then, this experience suggests that graduate teachers in foreign languages could profitably pursue networking by investigating formats and experience of the growing numbers of graduate classes in English that now regularly use network systems.

Implications for Research

The foregoing implementation suggestions are tentative at best because computer technologies are new and their applications will, presumably, open up new syntheses that merge extant teaching practices with innovative computer potential. Consequently, researchers face particular challenges posed by this potential. Extant research models and their premises may not reveal the full potential of computer use. In the sense that models frame research goals, the mode chosen can predict outcomes. Traditionally, experimental techniques compare gains or losses in specific skill areas among otherwise comparable control and experimental groups. Networking, however, introduces a myriad of variables that are hard to pin down: individual group dynamics, teacher management with regard to tasks, assessment and feedback, and variables in machinery, programs, and interface.

To create anything like a parallel curriculum for control and experimental groups, researchers will have to look carefully at the precise factors they wish to compare. With regard to self-reflective learning, will a study look at how the InterChange helps students become better monitors of their own language competencies? What are specific manifestations of that monitoring process, a goal stressed in several chapters in this volume? If the research concern is writing proficiency, which dimension of writing competence is sought: rhetorical elegance, grammatical accuracy, development of an individual student's voice, command of content, or communicative effectiveness (and how it is measured)? Such very different objectives have yet to be clearly differentiated by applied linguists who undertake research in English composition and foreign language learning.

Yet another research model, performance tracking, is enabled by our increasingly networked nation. Directly and indirectly, the chapters in this volume imply that such longitudinal projects are needed to see whether short-term gains become long-term benefits to learners. As computer classrooms become more common options for postsecondary schools across the country, long-term assessments that access and cross-check relevant databases will become practical realities. Studies that conduct tracking of foreign language students through their college years and subsequently could sort and follow the career trajectories of students with considerable computer experience alongside those who had relatively little or none. Such data might also yield feedback about possible correspondences between the learning curve of these students and computer use.

To assess longitudinal benefits between computer and non-computer groups, a study could compare such factors as language loss over a period of years, identify percentages of students continuing their language study beyond required courses, examine performance on standard achievements as well as criterion-referenced tests, and trace incidence of foreign language use in careers or for personal enrichment (reading, television viewing, e-mail abroad, tourism). Given the uniformly enthusiastic responses to InterChange reported by Beauvois and Jaeglin, such research might also want to check whether computer applications such as InterChange attract new students to a program and motivate their retention.

For teachers, networking provides a tool for research based on individual teaching and performance objectives. Its feedback capabilities, documented in this volume, are readily accessed by any instructor. Examination of transcripts provides precisely the kinds of information teachers want to assess student performance and their own pedagogies as well. Most word processing programs can tell teachers how many entries and the length of entries students make in a class hour. Features can check, for example, incidence of vocabulary use. The advent of technology in our daily lives and the looming promises of the information age pose new demands on first- and second-language teachers. During a period of rapid political and social change in the United States and elsewhere in the world, the need to join language literacy with computer literacy is emerging as a national and international mandate.

This volume has attempted to show ways to extend the enterprise of integrating new technology into extant curricula by documenting and analyzing the use of networked computers for teaching language learners who are unfamiliar in some degree with linguistic norms for the language in question. The lens provided here by teachers of second languages focuses acutely on the construction and structuring of written discourse, and learning is measured rather precisely in developmental increments. Successful performance is more easily monitored and documented than it is in English composition classes, where students come to class literate and practiced in both vocabulary and syntax of their native tongue. For English second-language and foreign language learners, markers can be designated by instructors and textbooks, whereas in English studies, given the turn to the social and the appreciation of a diversity displayed especially in language use, there is reluctance to specify the marks of "good" language use or successful language use as all usage evaluations become potential message inhibitors when student content is foregrounded.

Nevertheless, concepts such as discourse management may be more applicable to English composition classrooms than is currently the case. The managerial techniques presented in this volume may be worth examining as a means by which to assess the contribution that interactive writing makes to course goals, since often teachers in English studies classrooms find networking highly attractive and emotionally positive experiences, yet inconclusive as regards a specific contribution to their instructional goals.

For second and foreign language teachers, further research could look at features described in this volume. To note just a few potential lines for additional inquiry, Chun's longitudinal documentation of increasingly complex syntax and an increasing range of speech acts lends itself well to analysis of e-mail exchanges on several counts. As Kelm suggests, e-mail transcripts could reveal, for example, if the exchanges between students and authentic speakers resulted in tangible changes in student writing over time. E-mail of language students with, for example, Brazilians or Germans affords an opportunity to compare, at least on a case study basis, the progress in writing of students who correspond with their linguistic peers and progress among those who write to native speakers of a language. Comparison of *linguistic* features (the accuracy issue) in exchanges among students of a second language and linguistic features in exchanges among students and native speakers of that language offers an opportunity to explore the unresolved issue: Differences, if any, between linguistic development characteristic of peer exchanges and linguistic development characteristic when the language learner spends equivalent time communicating with a native speaker.

As spontaneous, largely unstructured messages, transcripts would also reveal *cultural* inquiries and insights that arise in the course of exchanges with peers and people in foreign countries. Given that many social or political references (e.g., to holidays, educational or business practices) are culture-bound, the researcher who looks at styles of teacher input or e-mail transcripts among students in different countries could assess the times that elaboration on such references was requested by participants in those exchanges. Transcripts also reveal the frequency with which *unfamiliar vocabulary or rhetorical features* occur and are the subject of subsequent discussion (the cognitive input issue). If the incidence of such entries were relatively frequent, the researcher might then want to note if curiosity promoted acquisition (i.e., if students would begin to incorporate these initially unfamiliar linguistic features into their second language use).

Theoretically at least, the *motivational characteristics* of a networking class documented by Beauvois and Jaeglin are a rich source for longitudinal study. Does, for example, contact with those actually living in the country whose language was being studied motivate more ongoing exchanges than contact with peers? Overall, do networking exchanges with peers and native speakers tend to be continued beyond the classroom? Do such exchanges foster other types of personal or professional contact in later life? How does such contact affect language retention or loss?

As a brief inventory for suggested research, these linguistic, cultural, motivational, and cognitive possibilities introduce a unique characteristic to the second-language classroom: The potential of the local area network and the Internet to extend that classroom beyond its traditional confines. With this capability, networking promises to expand not only pedagogical horizons, but also research purviews for language learning.

Acronyms Used in *Language Learning Online*

ACTFL	Association of College Teachers of Foreign Languages
AI	artificial intelligence
CACD	computer-assisted class discussion
CALICO	Computer-Assisted Language Instruction Consortium
CALL	computer-assisted language learning
CLP	communicative language proficiency
CMC	computer-mediated communication
CWRL	Computer Writing and Research Lab, University of Texas
DIWE	The Daedalus Integrated Writing Environment
ENFI	electronic networks for interaction
ESL	English as a second language
FL	foreign language
L1	first language
L2	second language
LAN	local area network
MLU	mean length of utterance
PC	personal computer
TA / AI	teaching assistant / assistant i191nstructor
TESOL	Teachers of English to Speakers of Other Languages
TOEFL	Test of English as a Foreign Language

Index

D

E

N

O

P

R

S

T

U

W

About the Contributors

Katherine Arens is a professor in the Dept. of Germanic Studies at the University of Texas, Austin. Her work spans the literary and intellectual history since the Enlightenment, with special emphasis on the philosophy and psychology of language, in theory and practice. Notable publications for readers of the present collection include *Reading for Meaning* (1991, with Janet Swaffar and Heidi Byrnes) and *Structures of Knowing: Psychologies of the 19th Century* (1989), as well as essays on issues of the teaching of L1 and L2 reading and writing in *Die Unterrichtspraxis*, *The Journal of General Education*, and *The Modern Language Journal*.

Margaret Healy Beauvois, M.A. in French from Middlebury College; Ph.D. in Foreign Language Education from the University of Texas, Austin, is Assistant Professor of French and Coordinator/Supervisor of First and Second Year Instruction in the Department of Romance and Asian Languages at the University of Tennessee - Knoxville. She is Chair of a campus-wide initiative to incorporate the use of computer networking into the curriculum across disciplines. Her area of research is computer-assisted communication and writing using local area networks. She also does teacher training in Cooperative Learning, the integration of video and CALL into the foreign language curriculum.

Dorothy M. Chun, Ph.D. University of California Berkeley, is Associate Professor of German at the University of California, Santa Barbara. Her main research areas are discourse intonation, second-language acquisition, and computer-assisted language learning. She has published in *The Modern Language Journal, Language Learning and Technology, Foreign Language Annals, Journal of Educational Multimedia and Hypermedia, CALICO Journal, Die Unterrichtspraxis* and is co-author of two multimedia readers, *CyberBuch* and *Ciberteca.*

Christophe Jaeglin was born in France in 1968 and has been studying european languages, history, translation and computer sciences. In 1988 he was studying on a scholarship at the C.-Albrechts Universität zu Kiel and in 1991 he obtained the 'Maîtrise' on the German Reunification with honors from the Université de Strasbourg. Between 1992 and 1994 he was appointed as an assistant instructor by the Dept. of Germanic Languages of the University of Texas, Austin, where he was given an opportunity to teach using a computer network, which led him to his 1994 M.A. Thesis, "Teaching Foreign Languages with a Network of Computers: CACD with the Daedalus InterChange Program." He translated parts of the work "History of Translation" for the FIT (Ed. UNESCO). He is currently teaching German and English in France and finishing his 'Doctorat' on "Die zweite Vergangenheitsbewältigung."

Orlando R. Kelm is associate professor of hispanic linguistics in the Department of Spanish and Portuguese at the University of Texas, Austin. He teaches courses in applied linguistics in both Spanish and Portuguese. His professional interests include language for special purposes, such as business language and computer-assisted language instruction. Dr. Kelm received his B.A. and M.A. from Brigham Young University and his Ph.D. from the University of California, Berkeley. Dr. Kelm may be reached at orkelm@mail.utexas.edu.

Phillip Markley has a Ph.D. in Applied Linguistics and is presently an Associate Professor at Ritsumeikan University in Kyoto, Japan. He has taught ESL on four continents and has done research in CALL for nearly 14 years beginning with managing and developing CALL programs for 17 ARAMCO schools in Saudi Arabia. He was also a panelist and coordinator of the TESOL CALL Academic Session for TESOL '96 and the coordinator of the same panel for TESOL '97. His other areas of research involve reading comprehension and reading strategies.

Susan Romano is an assistant professor of English at the University of Texas, San Antonio. She is interested in the pedagogies of online writing instruction, and her recent research examines the rhetorical means by which student participants in electronic conferences establish and refuse discussion topics and social identities. She has published articles on ethnicity and gender in online teaching environments, on writing program administration in the electronic age, and on composition research on the World Wide Web. Currently she is researching the Internet literacy practices of K-12 students in northern Mexico. Her 1993 "Egalitarianism Narrative" won the Ellen Nold Award for best article in computers and composition studies.

John Slatin has been teaching in networked computer environments since 1987, and has served as director of the internationally-acclaimed Computer Writing and Research Lab at University of Texas, Austin since 1989. As a member of the campus-wide Long Range Planning and Multimedia Instruction Committees and the Liberal Arts Faculty Computer Committee, Slatin has been directly involved in efforts to integrate technology and instruction on a large scale. He has also designed the nation's first Ph.D. specialization in Computers and English Studies, which enrolled its first students in Fall 1996. He is the author of "Reading Hypertext: Order and Coherence in a New Medium" (1990) and "Is Thre a Class in this Text? Creating Knowledge in the Electronic Classroom" (1992). His book, *This Will Change Everything: Computers and English Studies* will be published by Ablex. In 1996, Slatin was appointed director of the Institute for Technology and Learning at University of Texas, Austin.

Nancy Sullivan is Associate Professor of English at Texas A&M University, Corpus Christi. She teaches courses in language acquistion, sociolinguistics, freshman writing, and grammar. Her publications on computer-assisted language learning have appeared in *TESOL Journal* and *System*. Her current research interests include the examination of role of language background in remedial freshman writing classes. She has also been conducting a study in South Texas on categories of support and opposition to English language legislation.

Janet Swaffar is a Professor of German at the University of Texas, Austin. She works on applications of literary and linguistic theory to curricular and pedagogical concerns of first- and second-language learning. As a literary critic she has published on German literary magazines and nineteenth and twentieth century German narratives and dramas. In applied linguistics she has written about cultural literacy, reading, and media use. With Katherine Arens and Heidi Byrnes, her most recent book is *Reading for Meaning: An Integrated Approach*, a volume that identifies the strategic applications of extant literary and linguistic theories to the identification and analysis of the cultural and content systems in print and media texts. With Katherine Arens she has written a WWW site on reading for the AATG. This site illustrates how teachers can create tasks that reflect the Standards adopted by ACTFL (communication, connections, culture, comparison, communities), the FL profession's empowerment strategies reflected in the computer use described in *Language Learning Online*.